Collins

Year 6
Maths & English

Targeted Study
& Practice Book

Jon Goulding and Tom Hall

How to use this book

This Maths and English Study and Practice book contains everything children need for the school year in one book.

A **study page** and a **practice page** for each topic.

'**Remember**' boxes highlight key points

Key words highlighted on each Study page with definitions in the glossary.

Tips give ideas on how to remember key information.

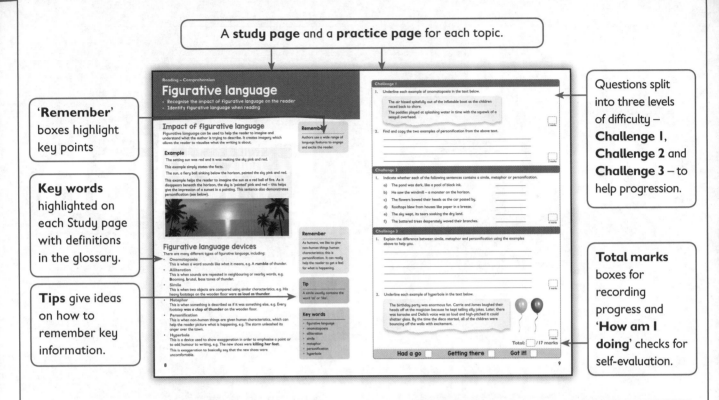

Questions split into three levels of difficulty – **Challenge 1**, **Challenge 2** and **Challenge 3** – to help progression.

Total marks boxes for recording progress and '**How am I doing**' checks for self-evaluation.

Six **Progress tests** included throughout the book for ongoing assessment and monitoring progress.

Mixed questions for maths and English test topics from throughout the book.

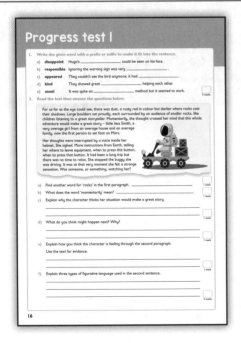

Problem-solving questions identified with a clear symbol.

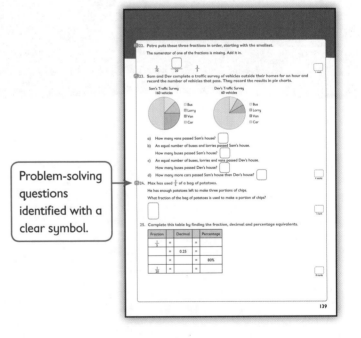

Answers provided for all the questions.

Contents

Root words, prefixes and suffixes

- Apply knowledge of the meaning of root words
- Apply knowledge of the meaning of prefixes and suffixes

Root words, prefixes and suffixes

A **root word** has meaning on its own before **prefixes** and **suffixes** are added.

A prefix is a letter or group of letters that can be added to the start of a root word. When adding a prefix, the spelling of the root word does not change. A prefix changes the meaning of the root word.

Example

> **mis-** (and **dis-**) give a negative or opposite meaning.

- **mis**treat (**mis-** + treat)
  *Some cruel people **mis**treat their pets.*

  > **super-** means 'to be above, over or beyond'. Supernatural means 'beyond natural'.

- **super**natural (**super-** + natural)
  *There was a **super**natural occurrence.*

  > **bi-** means 'two'. In this case it refers to two wheels.

- **bi**cycle (**bi-** + cycle)
  *She rode a racing **bi**cycle.*

  > **auto-** means 'self'. A self-written biography is an **auto**biography.

- **auto**biography (**auto-** + biography)
  *He wrote his **auto**biography.*

  > **pre-** means 'before'. In this case, before history (before humans).

- **pre**historic (**pre-** + historic)
  *They were bones of a **pre**historic beast.*

A suffix is a letter or group of letters that can be added to the end of a root word. In some cases, a suffix can be added to another suffix that has already been added. Sometimes, adding a suffix changes the spelling of the root word. The addition of a suffix also changes the meaning of the root word.

Example

treat**ment** (treat + **-ment**)

mistreat**ment** (mis- + treat + **-ment**)

explain (root word, verb)

explain + **-ation** ⇨ explanation

> The **verbs** 'treat' and 'mistreat' become **nouns** when the suffix **-ment** is added.

> The **i** is dropped from the root word when the suffix is added. Consider how the 'root' part of **explain** and **explan**ation sound different.

Care is needed when reading and pronouncing many words once the word ending has been altered, despite the root being the same.

Example

- **medic** and **medical** have a hard **c**. **medicine** and **medicinal** have a soft **c**.
- **sign** has a long **i** sound and a silent **g**; **signature** has a short **i** sound and the **g** is pronounced.
- **athlete** has a long **e** sound; **athletic** has a short **e** sound.

Knowledge of root words – their meaning and pronunciation – is important when reading and understanding texts. Sometimes pronunciation changes with changes to the root word. Look out for such words in texts you read.

Challenge 1

1. Write the root word for each of the words below.

   a) inexplicable _____

   b) signatory _____

   c) medicinally _____

   d) decomposition _____

   4 marks

Challenge 2

1. Explain the meaning of the prefix and the whole word for each example.

   a) misheard _____

   b) unbelievable _____

   c) impossible _____

   d) overheat _____

   e) biannual _____

   f) aerospace _____

   g) transplant _____

   14 marks

Challenge 3

1. Add an appropriate prefix or suffix to each word to complete the sentence.

   a) port   They had to find a way to _____ the furniture back home.

   b) scribe   She decided to _____ medicine for the patient.

   c) excite   There was much _____ after the goal.

   d) misinform   The police received a lot of _____ about the accident.

   e) human   The flying character in the film had _____ powers.

   5 marks

2. Six of the words in the text below have the wrong prefix. Underline each of these and write the correct words in the box below the text.

   > On arrival at the museum there was an imbelievable commotion as they had discalculated the number of tickets they had needed. They had unsufficient money to buy extra tickets and were inallowed entry. Instead, they decided to go to the park. On arrival at the park, they uncovered that there was a live concert.
   >
   > The music was loud and their own voices became disaudible.

   6 marks

   Total: ____ /29 marks

Had a go ☐   **Getting there** ☐   **Got it!** ☐

Formal and informal language

- Recognise the difference between Standard English and non-Standard English
- Recognise the difference between formal and informal language

Standard and non-Standard English

Standard English is the form of English that is generally accepted as correct. **Non-Standard English** is the form of English that doesn't follow the rules of grammar.

Example

It will not rain tomorrow. ← Standard English

It ain't gonna rain tomorrow. ← Non-Standard English

Formal and informal language

Written and spoken English can be **formal** or **informal**. This is dependent on the words that are used and how they are written or spoken.

When using formal language, full and correct versions of words or phrases are used and **contractions** such as 'can't' are rare. Formal language (particularly in non-fiction writing) may use subject-specific and often technical words.

Example

The seashore has lots of junk from the sea. ← Informal

The shoreline is littered with flotsam and jetsam. ← Formal

Formal language should be used when speaking or writing to somebody you do not know, or somebody in authority, such as a teacher.

Informal language is used when you are writing to or speaking to people you know well, such as your friends and family. Informal language might include contractions and slang, and sometimes words are omitted from sentences.

Example

Formal	Informal
Recipient addressed officially. → Dear Miss Green,	Hey mate, soz, but can't come to your party after school on Thursday. Got to go hospital. ← Slang: 'soz' rather than 'sorry'.
'will not' rather than 'won't'. → I am writing to let you know that Natasha will not be in school on Thursday as she has an appointment at the eye hospital.	← Contraction – 'can't'.
Reason given with some detail. →	← Missing words – 'I've', 'to the'.
Signed off with 'Yours sincerely'. → Yours sincerely, Mr Mike Jones	See ya soon, Tash ← Friendly sign-off and slang ('ya').

In story writing, the language used is generally formal. But, when a character is speaking, think about the language they would use – there may need to be a switch to informal for dialogue. Spoken language is generally far less formal than written language.

Remember

We speak and write to friends and family in an informal way but a letter to the Head Teacher or writing in an exam would use formal language.

Key words

- Standard English
- non-Standard English
- formal
- informal
- contraction

6

Challenge 1

1. Write F or I next to each word or phrase to indicate whether it is formal (F) or informal (I) language.

   a) Dear Sir ☐

   b) Cheers mate ☐

   c) isn't ☐

   d) is not ☐

   e) Hiya ☐

   f) Yours faithfully ☐

   ☐ 6 marks

Challenge 2

1. Read the two passages below.

   a) It is a wonderful place. There are several activities for children and adults. This ensures everybody can participate.

   Safety equipment such as helmets and harnesses are compulsory for some attractions but these are readily available, which keeps queuing to a minimum.

   b) It's an ace place. There's loads to do for kids and grown-ups so everyone can take part.

   You have to wear safety stuff to do some activities. There are loads of them though so you don't have to wait long.

   Write formal or informal for each passage, and say who or what each passage may have been written for.

   a) _____

   b) _____

   ☐ 4 marks

Challenge 3

1. Compare **three** ideas from each passage in Challenge 2 that tells you whether it is formal or informal. One has been done for you.

Formal	Informal
wonderful	*ace*

   ☐ 3 marks

2. Write these sentences in Standard English.

   a) I'd love the job cos I'd be fab at it.

   _____

   _____

   b) One man were punching the other, it was a proper brawl.

   _____

   _____

   ☐ 2 marks

   Total: ☐ / 15 marks

   Had a go ☐   **Getting there** ☐   **Got it!** ☐

7

Figurative language

- Recognise the impact of figurative language on the reader
- Identify figurative language when reading

Impact of figurative language

Figurative language can be used to help the reader to imagine and understand what the author is trying to describe. It creates imagery which allows the reader to visualise what the writing is about.

Example

The setting sun was red and it was making the sky pink and red.

This example simply states the facts.

The sun, a fiery ball sinking below the horizon, painted the sky pink and red.

This example helps the reader to imagine the sun as a red ball of fire. As it disappears beneath the horizon, the sky is 'painted' pink and red – this helps give the impression of a sunset in a painting. This sentence also demonstrates personification (see below).

Figurative language devices

There are many different types of figurative language, including:

- **Onomatopoeia**
  This is when a word sounds like what it means, e.g. A **rumble** of thunder.
- **Alliteration**
  This is when sounds are repeated in neighbouring or nearby words, e.g. **B**ooming, **b**rutal, **b**ass tones of thunder.
- **Simile**
  This is when two objects are compared using similar characteristics, e.g. His heavy footsteps on the wooden floor were **as loud as thunder**.
- **Metaphor**
  This is when something is described as if it was something else, e.g. Every footstep **was a clap of thunder** on the wooden floor.
- **Personification**
  This is when non-human things are given human characteristics, which can help the reader picture what is happening, e.g. The storm unleashed its anger over the town.
- **Hyperbole**
  This is a device used to show exaggeration in order to emphasise a point or to add humour to writing, e.g. The new shoes were **killing her feet**.

  This is exaggeration to basically say that the new shoes were uncomfortable.

1. Underline each example of onomatopoeia in the text below.

> The air hissed spitefully out of the inflatable boat as the children raced back to shore.
>
> The paddles played at splashing water in time with the squawk of a seagull overhead.

3 marks

2. Find and copy the two examples of personification from the above text.

_____

_____

_____

_____

2 marks

1. Indicate whether each of the following sentences contains a simile, metaphor or personification.

   a)   The pond was dark, like a pool of black ink.   _____

   b)   He saw the windmill – a monster on the horizon.   _____

   c)   The flowers bowed their heads as the car passed by.   _____

   d)   Rooftops blew from houses like paper in a breeze.   _____

   e)   The sky wept, its tears soaking the dry land.   _____

   f)   The battered trees desperately waved their branches.   _____

6 marks

1. Explain the difference between simile, metaphor and personification using the examples above to help you.

_____

_____

_____

_____

_____

_____

3 marks

2. Underline each example of hyperbole in the text below.

> The birthday party was enormous fun. Carrie and James laughed their heads off at the magician because he kept telling silly jokes. Later, there was karaoke and Della's voice was so loud and high-pitched it could shatter glass. By the time the disco started, all of the children were bouncing off the walls with excitement.

3 marks

Total: [ ] **/ 17 marks**

Had a go [ ]   **Getting there** [ ]   **Got it!** [ ]

9

Fiction

- Demonstrate an understanding of fiction texts
- Draw inferences from the text about a character

Understanding the text

Fiction texts include stories and poems of many different genres, themes and ideas. Fiction is made-up. When reading a fiction text, it is important to understand what the author is trying to say about characters, settings and plot.

Description and figurative language

In descriptive passages, an author might use a range of **adjectives**, **adverbs** and **figurative language** to 'paint' a vivid picture of the character, setting or events.

Example

> She liked the lake because it was peaceful and she liked the boats and mountains. It was a nice and safe place.

> She was attracted to the lake by the calm and the peace. Sitting there, she took delight in the way yachts glided silently by against the backdrop of mountains standing on guard, surrounding and protecting the blue waters. She needed this contrast with her usual daily life. She lay back on the grass, closed her eyes and allowed a hint of a smile to change the shape of her lips.

Meaning of words and inference

It is important to be able to use **inference** to help understand a character's thoughts, feelings and actions.

Example

What can we **infer** about the reason for the character being attracted by the 'calm and the peace' in the text above?

It would be easy for the author to write, 'the lake made her happy because she liked the peace as her usual daily life was hectic.' However, inference is needed to see that later in the passage, 'She needed this contrast with her daily life.' The word 'contrast' helps us to infer that her daily life was the opposite of calm and peaceful.

What do the words 'she took delight' mean in the text above?

Looking at the meaning of words such as 'contrast' and thinking about what the author is implying helps us to infer more about the character and the scene. In this case, 'she took delight' suggests she sat there enjoying watching the yachts, the mountains and the lake.

What can the reader infer about the character from the last sentence in the text above?

The fact that she 'lay back on the grass' and 'closed her eyes' infers that she was relaxed. 'A hint of a smile' infers a feeling of happiness.

It is also important to recognise why the author uses certain devices in a text. Think about the author's intent.

Example

How does the author suggest that the lake is a safe place in the text above?

The use of personification – the 'mountains standing on guard' – almost gives the feeling that the mountains are like soldiers 'protecting' the scene.

Remember

Think about what the author is trying to say. Use a dictionary if you are unsure about some of the vocabulary.

These words, while true for the character, do not really help the reader imagine the scene.

These words provide more description and make it easier to imagine the scene and the character in it. Notice the use of adverbs, adjectives and **personification** to enhance the description.

Key words

- fiction
- adjective
- adverb
- figurative language
- inference
- personification

1. Find and copy an adverb and an adjective from the second example text on the opposite page and explain why you think each is used.

   a) adverb _____

   _____

   b) adjective _____

   _____

Read the text then answer Challenges 2 and 3 below.

There was mud and there was mud. A dirty track, a soggy field or a few murky puddles were one thing, but this was heavy, sticky and deep. A swamp of treacle lay where the road had once been. The road itself could be under there, he thought, but then again, it had probably been washed away by the flood like everything else. All but the thickest trees lay like fallen soldiers. Strong, stone walls had been whisked away by the water. As he tried to lift first one foot, then the other, wading towards the field, he could already see a far smaller herd than usual. He knew, and his heart sank. He swallowed hard and fought back tears.

1. a) What metaphor is used to describe the mud?

   _____

   b) What simile is used in the text?

   _____

2. a) Why do you think a 'dirty track', 'soggy field' and 'murky puddles' are mentioned at the beginning of the second sentence before the author writes 'but this was heavy, sticky and deep'?

   _____

   _____

   b) What is the effect of using the word 'strong' in the sentence, 'Strong, stone walls had been whisked away by the water'?

   _____

   _____

1. a) Who might the person in the text be?

   _____

   b) Why do you think the character 'swallowed hard and fought back tears'?

   Use evidence from the text to support your answer.

   _____

   _____

   _____

Total: [ ] /8 marks

Had a go [ ]   **Getting there** [ ]   **Got it!** [ ]

Poetry

- Demonstrate an understanding of poetry, including structure, rhyme and interpretation

Structure and rhyming

Poems can be structured in many different ways. Some poems have specific **rhyming patterns** with certain lines rhyming with others. Some poems have little structure and/or do not rhyme at all. These are described as **free verse**.

Retrieving information from poetry

Even more so than other fiction, poetry uses **figurative language** to stimulate the imagination of the reader and convey feelings and emotions.

Example

Anticipation

Butterflies and stomach churning,

Impatient fidgeting and pacing,

Clock watching, silent yearning,

A car outside, heart quickly racing,

Door handle, slowly turning,

Then, joy and finally embracing.

> **Remember**
>
> Poems have different structures, such as haiku (5 syllables in line 1, 7 syllables in line 2 and 5 syllables in line 3) or limericks which are 5-line humorous poems.

> Poem title – 'Anticipation', which means looking forward to something.

> Butterflies is often used to describe excitement or nervousness. The person in the poem is waiting, yearning for somebody to return.

> Alternate lines rhyme in this poem – an **ABAB** pattern; 'churning' rhymes with 'yearning', 'pacing' with 'racing'.

A variety of questions could be asked about the above poem, focusing on the words chosen by the author, such as:

- What do the words 'Impatient fidgeting and pacing' tell us?
  The character is clearly nervous or excited.

- Why do you think the words 'heart quickly racing' are used?
  They show the build-up in excitement or action at hearing a car outside.

Poetry does not always have to be serious. It can also contain humour.

Example

Lunchtime Disaster

A tide of orange,

A slow wave across the surface,

Carrying many helpless, silent souls,

As the sauce and beans flow,

Over the edge of the plate,

And onto the table!

> The title suggests something bad happens.

> A **metaphor** for the sauce!

> **Personification** of baked beans.

> No rhyming pattern.

> The first three lines make the reader wonder what's happening. The final three lines give it away.

Questions about this poem could also centre around the author's language:
- What is the author comparing the sauce to in this poem?
  It implies that it is like the sea by using words like 'tide' and 'wave'.
- How is personification used?
  It makes the beans seem like helpless, silent people.

> **Key words**
>
> - poem
> - rhyming pattern
> - figurative language
> - metaphor
> - personification

Read the poem then answer Challenge 1 and Challenge 2.

Galloping

Race across mountain and plain,
Riding through the wind and rain.
A deserted barn to sleep and rest,
Days and nights moving west.
Enemy closer day by day,
Should we move or should we stay?
Decision made, we sat and sighed,
Then onwards with our galloping ride.

Challenge 1

1. Which lines in this poem rhyme with each other?

   _____

   1 mark

2. Continue the rhyming pattern by selecting appropriate words to complete the missing endings of the next four lines of the poem.

   Across dry desert on the run

   Beneath the fierce sweltering _____

   At last the shade of wiry trees

   And a cooler, softly blowing _____

   2 marks

Challenge 2

1. Explain what you think the poem is about.

   _____

   _____

   _____

   1 mark

Challenge 3

1. Read the Haiku poem below.

   Mist

   Silently creeping
   Graceful white sheet on meadows
   A haunting beauty

   a) Give an example of the use of personification in the Haiku poem.

      _____

   b) Give an example of the use of metaphor in the Haiku poem.

      _____

      2 marks

Total: [ ] /6 marks

Had a go [ ]   **Getting there** [ ]   **Got it!** [ ]

Non-fiction

- Demonstrate an understanding of non-fiction texts, including presentation, structure and language

Presentation and information

Non-fiction texts are factual: they contain facts and information.

While parts of a non-fiction text will be written in sentences and paragraphs, some information may be presented as pictures and diagrams, tables or graphs, bullet point lists and in 'information' or 'fact' boxes.

Example

Learn Guitar

The guitar is a great instrument to play and the basics are easy to learn.

Getting started

An acoustic guitar is often considered best for a beginner, although an electric guitar can be used. Find a teacher or an online course.

The basics

First, find out about the parts:

- body
- neck
- frets
- strings
- tuning pegs

Acoustic guitar

Next, learn how to hold the guitar.

> **Did you know?**
> Most guitars have six strings but some can have 12.
> Bass guitars usually have four strings.

> **Famous guitarists**
> - Bob Dylan (folk)
> - Slash (rock)
> - John Williams (classical)
> - Chuck Berry (rock and roll)

Discussions and questions about non-fiction texts often focus on organisational features as well as language features.

Example

- What is the purpose of the two fact boxes in the text above?
  These give further information and facts to the reader, adding extra interest.
- How is the text under the sub-heading 'The basics' organised?
  As instructions using time adverbs such as 'first' and 'next' and bullet points.

Different non-fiction texts will be presented differently, with different structures. Texts of the same genre may also be very different.

- An **instruction text** will usually consist of steps. Many also include pictures to go with each step. Recipes often have a picture of the finished dish.
- A **recount** is usually organised into paragraphs in chronological order. Sometimes, groups of paragraphs may appear under different sub-headings for different parts of the recount. Photographs may also be used.
- **Newspaper articles** often use short, snappy headlines for the whole text and different paragraphs. They are written in the third person and past tense.
- **Persuasive texts** will include information to persuade the reader about something. Rhetorical questions and emotional language may be added.

Remember

Non-fiction texts share information about a topic, or specific aspects of a topic. They generally contain facts.

The main part of the text is written in paragraphs.

Subject-specific vocabulary is used.

Subheadings give ideas of what each part of the text is about.

Additional information is provided in fact boxes.

Bullet points make key information easy to find.

A **rhetorical question** is used ('Did you know?') They are not intended to be answered but simply to make a point – in this case, that different guitars have different numbers of strings.

Tip

Non-fiction texts often use subject-specific vocabulary. You might need to use the book's glossary or a dictionary to find the meaning of some words.

Key words

- non-fiction
- subject-specific vocabulary
- rhetorical question

Read the text and then answer the Challenges.

Running Inspiration

Roger Bannister was an English athlete who became famous as the first person to run one mile in less than four minutes. For many years, the 'four-minute-mile' had inspired athletes to try to break that remarkable time barrier.

What will inspire you?

You don't have to be trying to break the four-minute-mile to start running.

People start running for many reasons:

- To get fit
- To enjoy the fresh air
- To make friends
- To challenge themselves

What do you need?

The beauty of running is that you need very little. A pair of trainers and some sportswear is enough to start with.

Challenge 1

1. a) What do you think the phrase 'remarkable time barrier' means?

   _____

   b) Why are bullet points used in the text?

   _____

   2 marks

Challenge 2

1. Tick two options that would fit with the text as the next sub-heading.

   Getting started ☐   Swimming ☐

   Winning races ☐   Roger Bannister ☐

   Warming up ☐

   2 marks

2. Explain your choices from above.

   _____

   _____

   1 mark

Challenge 3

1. Explain whether each fact box below would be suitable to go with the text 'Running Inspiration'.

   Bannister broke the record in 1954. Many athletes were inspired to take on this challenge after hearing of Bannister's achievement.

   _____
   _____
   _____

   The Olympic Games are held every four years. There are running races over many distances.

   _____
   _____
   _____

   2 marks

Total: ☐ /7 marks

Had a go ☐   **Getting there** ☐   **Got it!** ☐

Progress test I

1. **Write the given word with a prefix or suffix to make it fit into the sentence.**

   a) **disappoint**   Hugo's _____ could be seen on his face.

   b) **responsible**   Ignoring the warning sign was very _____ .

   c) **appeared**   They couldn't see the bird anymore; it had _____ .

   d) **kind**   They showed great _____ helping each other.

   e) **usual**   It was quite an _____ method but it seemed to work.

   5 marks

2. **Read the text then answer the questions below.**

   For as far as the eye could see, there was dust, a rusty red in colour but darker where rocks cast their shadows. Large boulders sat proudly, each surrounded by an audience of smaller rocks, like children listening to a great storyteller. Momentarily, the thought crossed her mind that this whole adventure would make a great story – little Jess Smith, a very average girl from an average house and an average family, now the first person to set foot on Mars.

   Her thoughts were interrupted by a voice inside her helmet. She sighed. More instructions from Earth, telling her where to leave equipment, when to press this button, when to press that button. It had been a long trip but there was no time to relax. She stopped the buggy she was driving. It was at that very moment she felt a strange sensation. Was someone, or something, watching her?

   a) Find another word for 'rocks' in the first paragraph. _____

   1 mark

   b) What does the word 'momentarily' mean? _____

   1 mark

   c) Explain why the character thinks her situation would make a great story.

   _____

   _____

   1 mark

   d) What do you think might happen next? Why?

   _____

   _____

   1 mark

   e) Explain how you think the character is feeling through the second paragraph.

   Use the text for evidence.

   _____

   _____

   1 mark

   f) Explain three types of figurative language used in the second sentence.

   _____

   _____

   _____

   3 marks

3. Rewrite the given root word with a prefix, suffix or both to complete each sentence.

a) The trip to the castle was most **(enjoy)** _____.

b) Her mum said she was **(sense)** _____ teasing her brother when he was poorly.

c) The doctor said the **(medic)** _____ would have her back on her feet soon.

d) The mistakes made in the test were **(explain)** _____.

e) In the test, they had to add a **(fix)** _____ to each word.

4. Six of the words in the text below have the wrong prefix. Underline each of these and write the correct words in the box below the text.

> They had been set an almost unpossible task. To start with, the clue was very nearly inlegible. Once they had uncoded it they then realised that they only had two hours to cover 10 miles on foot. Sam suggested using their motor scooters but they were delegal on public roads. It was then that Jess came up with an idea. It was quite inusual but she was known for her imconventional thinking.

5. Write F or I next to each word or phrase to indicate whether it is formal (F) or informal (I) language.

a) Cheers ☐

b) That's brill ☐

c) Yours sincerely ☐

d) Please do not ☐

e) Please refrain ☐

f) See ya ☐

6. **Read the text and answer the questions.**

The hunters of the unexplained

From visiting aliens and strange lake monsters to things that go bump in the night – people love a good mystery or ghost story. But surely they're not true. Or are they?

Hunters

There are people who dedicate their lives to finding the truth about mysteries. Many claim they have seen UFOs (Unidentified Flying Objects), ghosts and other strange things. They are hunters of the unexplained. Even if they have not seen anything themselves – and unsurprisingly, many have not – they put together the stories of others to help them understand the mystery.

Eyes, ears and lots of equipment

As well as looking and listening, modern mystery hunters use specialist equipment in their search. Computers, cameras and other devices help them detect unusual events. They then try to explain what has been witnessed.

Brave and patient

Would you be brave enough to hunt ghosts and monsters? You might also need to be very patient, sitting around waiting for something to happen, or not, as the case may be.

Craig Lewis has spent the past 12 years living in an old camper van on the shores of Loch Ness in Scotland. Every day he keeps an eye open for the famed Loch Ness Monster. He's not seen it yet but he is sure it exists!

The supposed 'Nessie'.

Unsolved mysteries

- The Yeti – a giant, snow creature (Himalayas)
- Loch Ness Monster – A large lake monster (Scotland)
- Area 51 – alien spacecraft (USA)
- The Bermuda Triangle – a place where ships and planes disappear

a) Why do you think the phrase 'things that go bump in the night' is used at the beginning of the text?

_____

b) Find in the third paragraph another word for 'seen'.

_____

c) What other title could be used for the fact box 'Unsolved Mysteries'?

_____

d) What opinion do you think the author has of these mysteries? Explain your answer using evidence from the text.

_____

_____

_____

4 marks

7. **Write the root word for each of the words below.**

   a) mistreatment _____

   b) international _____

   c) rediscovered _____

   d) impassable _____

4 marks

8. **Indicate whether each of the following sentences contains a simile, metaphor or personification.**

   a) Sophie crept along the hallway, as quiet as a mouse. _____

   b) Reflections of golden sunlight danced on the ceiling. _____

   c) The engine chatted away to itself in an almost familiar language. _____

   d) Jimmy rode with a straight back like a proud soldier on parade. _____

   e) The rocket, a strange white stick pointing skywards, was visible on the horizon.

   _____

5 marks

9. **Find and copy the examples of hyperbole from the text below.**

   It had been a long day. They had been up since sunrise and now, at nightfall, they were struggling. Adam was so hungry he could eat a horse. They had been walking forever (because Dave was now walking slower than a snail) and had covered about a million miles. Soon, though, they would be home and they could hardly wait.

   _____

   _____

   _____

4 marks

10. **Read this poem and then answer the questions.**

   My garden roses long ago
   Have perished from the leaf-strewn walks;
   Their pale, fair sisters smile no more
   Upon the sweet-brier stalks.

   a) What type of rhyming pattern does the poem have? Tick the correct answer.

   AABB ☐   ABAB ☐   ABCB ☐   ABCD ☐

   b) What type of figurative language is used in this poem to describe the roses?

   _____

   c) What is meant by 'perished' in the second line?

   _____

3 marks

Total: ☐ /50 marks

Place value, comparing and ordering numbers

- Know the value of each digit in a number up to 10,000,000
- Order and compare numbers up to 10,000,000

Place value

Every digit in a number has a **place value**.

Example

Here are column titles showing the value of the digits in the number 3,604,780

Millions	Hundreds of thousands	Tens of thousands	Thousands	Hundreds	Tens	Ones
3	6	0	4	7	8	0

In the number 3,604,780 there are three millions, 6 hundreds of thousands, 4 thousands, 7 hundreds and 8 tens.

The zeros are **place holders**. They are needed to make sure each digit sits in the correct column.

You would read this number as: three million, six hundred and four thousand, seven hundred and eighty.

Comparing and ordering numbers

Use place value to compare and order numbers. The greater the place value, the greater the number.

In the number 6,000,000 there are six millions; in the number 5,999,999 there are only 5 millions, so 6,000,000 must be the larger number.

Example

Use the symbols, **<** or **>** to compare 6,918,753 and 6,924,095

Both numbers have six millions and nine hundred thousands. The next most significant figure will be the tens of thousands, therefore:

6,918,753 < 6,924,095

This number has 1 ten of thousands, which makes it smaller than the second number, which has 2 tens of thousands.

Ordering numbers involves comparing more than two numbers.

Example

Look at these numbers:

4,826,710   4,716,469   4,709,811   4,825,915

Again, the place value of the digits is used to put them in order, starting with the smallest:

4,709,811   4,716,469   4,825,915   4,826,710

Challenge 1

1. **1,298,473**

   In the number above, find the value of:

   a) the digit 2 _____

   b) the digit 8 _____

   c) the digit 1 _____

   3 marks

2. Write these numbers in order starting with the smallest.

   | 672,821 | 673,897 | 672,348 | 673,901 | 673,187 |

   _____ _____ _____ _____ _____

   1 mark

3. Add **<** or **>** to complete the number sentences.

   a) 629,362 ☐ 629,632

   b) 1,843,318 ☐ 1,839,200

   2 marks

Challenge 2

1. Circle the number that has a digit 4 with a value of four hundred thousand.

   4,005,812   940,027   4,005   1,340,087   1,491,226

   1 mark

2. a) 275,843 + twenty thousand = _____

   b) 3,728,910 − two hundred thousand = _____

   c) 7,390,190 + six hundred thousand = _____

   3 marks

3. Write these numbers in order starting with the smallest.

   1,034,792   1,035,023   1,034,765   1,035,256   1,034,543

   _____ _____ _____ _____ _____

   1 mark

Challenge 3

PS 1. Lexie writes a sequence of numbers starting at 1,825,000. The sequence adds numbers in steps of fifty thousand.

   What will be the fifth number after 1,825,000?

   _____

   1 mark

PS 2. Samir has a secret number. He says, "In my number, the millions digit is 6, the hundreds digit is 8, the tens digit is 9, the hundreds of thousands digit is 7 and the thousands digit is 5."

   What could Samir's number be?

   _____

   1 mark

PS 3. Meena partitions some numbers in different ways. Tick the largest number.

35 thousands and 623 ones	346 hundreds and 57 ones	3,402 tens and 6 ones	357 hundreds	34 thousands and 7 hundreds
☐	☐	☐	☐	☐

   1 mark

   Total: ☐ / 14 marks

Had a go ☐   **Getting there** ☐   **Got it!** ☐

21

Reading, writing and rounding numbers

- Read and write numbers up to 10,000,000
- Round any number to a required degree of accuracy

Reading and writing numbers

This number is less than ten million:

7,924,684

It has two **commas**. These are useful when reading the number. Where the first comma is, say 'million' and where the second comma is say 'thousand'. So, this number is:

**seven million, nine hundred and twenty-four thousand,
six hundred and eighty-four**

Here is a large number written in words:

Two million, thirty-six thousand, five hundred and nine

Commas are used where the words 'million' and 'thousand' are said. So:

2,036,509

When writing a large number, remember the digits are written in groups of three. In the example immediately above, **place holder** zeros are needed before the '36' and between the '5' and '9' to make these groups of three, and to make sure each digit is in the correct **place value** column.

Rounding numbers

A number can be rounded up or rounded down to indicate which number it is closest to. The number it is rounded to is usually a **power of ten**, such as the nearest 10, 100, 1,000 and so on.

Example

5,648 rounded to the nearest thousand is 6,000

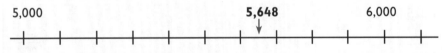

5,648 rounded to the nearest hundred is 5,600

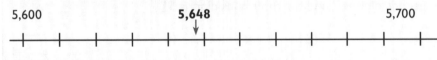

5,648 rounded to the nearest ten is 5,650

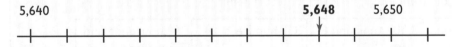

Numbers could be rounded in other ways too, even to the nearest 25.

5,648 to the nearest twenty-five is 5,650

Challenge 1

1. Circle **six hundred and two thousand, four hundred and seventy** written in digits.

   6,247   62,470   60,247   602,470   6,002,470

2. Write in digits:

   a) two hundred and fourteen thousand, six hundred and forty-two. _____

   b) nine hundred and fifteen thousand, six hundred and thirty-two _____

3. Round 381,726

   a) to the nearest 100 _____   b) to the nearest 10,000 _____

PS 4. A crowd at a rugby match was recorded in a newspaper as 16,000 but this number had been rounded to the nearest thousand. Circle the possible sizes of the actual crowd.

   15,798   16,498   15,498   15,598   16,698

Challenge 2

1. Write in digits:

   a) one million, two hundred and five thousand, nine hundred and fifteen _____

   b) three million, six hundred and eleven thousand, two hundred _____

2. Write in words:

   a) 2,809,000 _____

   b) 7,105,830 _____

3. Round 7,692,382

   a) to the nearest 1,000 _____   b) to the nearest 1,000,000 _____

Challenge 3

1. Add **<** or **>** to complete the number sentences.

   a) three million, six hundred thousand and one hundred ☐ 3,060,100

   b) 7,810,009 ☐ seven million, eight hundred and nine thousand and sixty-seven

   c) nine million, seventy thousand and thirty-five ☐ 9,700,035

PS 2. Jay puts two sets of three numbers in order. One number is missing from each set. What could these numbers be?

   a) 7,099,997 _____ 7,100,002   b) 5,450,000 _____ 5,460,000

PS 3. A number is rounded to 5,900,000

   If the number was rounded:

   a) to the nearest 10, what is the smallest number it could have been? _____

   b) to the nearest 100,000, what is the smallest number it could have been? _____

   c) to the nearest 10,000, what is the smallest number it could have been? _____

Total: ☐ /20 marks

Had a go ☐   Getting there ☐   Got it! ☐

Negative numbers

- Calculate numbers across 0
- Solve word problems involving negative numbers

Addition and subtraction with negative numbers

Negative numbers are numbers less than 0.

Example

17 – 25 =

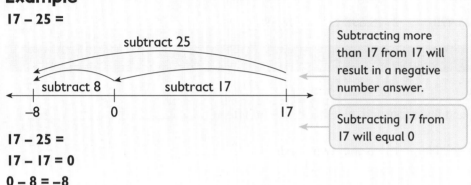

Subtracting more than 17 from 17 will result in a negative number answer.

Subtracting 17 from 17 will equal 0

17 – 25 =
17 – 17 = 0
0 – 8 = –8

Remember

Until you are confident completing calculations mentally, use a number line as an aid.

Example

What is the difference between –6 and 13?

This can be worked out by counting on in two steps: counting –6 to 0 and then counting the rest to reach 13

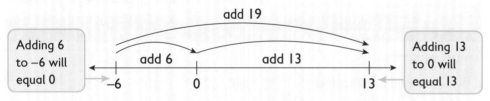

Adding 6 to –6 will equal 0

Adding 13 to 0 will equal 13

6 + 13 = 19 so the difference between –6 and 13 is **19**

Word problems

Once you have carefully read a word problem involving negative numbers, calculate the answer to the question using the addition and subtraction methods shown above.

Example

The highest temperature recorded in London between 1980 and 2010 was 37 °C.

The lowest temperature recorded in London between 1980 and 2010 was –12 °C.

What was the difference between the two temperatures?

$$-12 + ⓘ₂ = 0 \qquad 0 + ㉃₇ = 37 \qquad 12 + 37 = 49$$

So the difference between the two temperatures is **49 °C**

Key word

- negative number

Challenge 1

1. a) $6 - 9 =$ _____

    b) $2 - 9 =$ _____

    c) $7 - 10 =$ _____

    d) $-2 + 4 =$ _____

    e) $-4 + 9 =$ _____

    f) $-5 + 7 =$ _____

    6 marks

PS 2. The temperature outside is 6 °C. Overnight the temperature falls 8 °C.

What is the overnight temperature? _____

1 mark

PS 3. Max reads the temperature on the thermometer. The temperature falls by 11 °C.

What will the new temperature be? _____

1 mark

Challenge 2

1. a) $15 - 23 =$ _____

    b) $23 - 27 - 14 =$ _____

    c) $9 - 17 - 7 =$ _____

    d) $-12 + 26 =$ _____

    e) $-16 + 7 + 21 =$ _____

    f) $-9 + 16 =$ _____

    6 marks

PS 2. Circle the numbers that have the greatest difference.

-7 and 4   -12 and -2   3 and -7   10 and 2   -9 and -21

1 mark

PS 3. Circle the **two** numbers that have a difference of 15.

-10   -7   -4   3   8   15

1 mark

Challenge 3

PS 1. Find the number that is halfway between -16 and 8 _____

1 mark

PS 2. 14 and two different numbers have a difference of 30. One of the numbers is 44

What is the other number? _____

1 mark

PS 3. At 4:00 p.m. the temperature was 5 °C, but by 5:00 a.m. the temperature had fallen by 9 °C.

At 2:00 p.m. the temperature had risen to 3 °C.

By how many degrees had the temperature risen from 5:00 a.m. to 2:00 p.m.? _____

1 mark

PS 4. Find the missing numbers.

a) _____ $+ 17 - 4 = 2$ b) $-15 +$ _____ $- 6 = 12$

c) $12 - 17 -$ _____ $= -18$ d) $12 - 20 +$ _____ $= 0$

4 marks

Total: [ ] /23 marks

Had a go [ ]   **Getting there** [ ]   **Got it!** [ ]

25

Word problems

- Solve word problems with two or more steps

Solving word problems

For all word problems, read the problem carefully to work out what the question is asking. Many problems have more than one step that you need to work through before you can find the answer.

Example

The table shows the number of people that attended the first three football matches of two teams in one season.

	Game 1	Game 2	Game 3
United	25,286	29,417	30,739
City	31,466	27,287	32,408

How many more people attended the matches at City than at United across the three games?

1. Find the total of people at the United games.	2. Find the total of people at the City games.	3. Find the difference between the two totals.

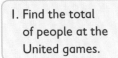

```
    2 5 2 8 6          3 1 4 6 6           8  ⁰0    5
    2 9 4 1 7          2 7 2 8 7         ⁷8̷ ⁴5̷ ¹1 ¹3̷6̷ ¹1
  + 3 0 7 3 9        + 3 2 4 0 8       −  8 5 4 4 2
    8 5 4 4 2          9 1 1 6 1          5 7 1 9
    1 1 1 2            1 1 1 2
```

Answer: 5,719 more people attended the City games than the United games.

Remember that not all problems need a 'story'.

Example

The **operation** signs are missing from this calculation. What are the missing signs?

5,067 ☐ 1,780 ☐ 3,825 ☐ 4,163 = 2,949

This problem could be solved by a 'trial and error' or 'trial and improvement' method by using addition and subtraction of the numbers until the answer of 2,949 is reached.

5,000 ☐ 2,000 ☐ 4,000 ☐ 4,000 =

5,067 − 1,780 + 3,825 − 4,163 = 2,949

Answer: The missing signs are **−, +, −** (in that order).

> Different trials will lead to 5,000 − 2,000 + 4,000 − 4,000 = 3,000 and testing this trial will give the correct answer.

> **Tip**
>
> Look at the words in the question: 'how many more', 'how many less' and 'what's the difference' often mean subtraction is involved; 'what is the total' and 'altogether' often mean addition is involved.

> Rounding the numbers to the nearest thousand allows easier mental trials.

> **Key word**
>
> - operation

PS 1. A printer produces 8,000 leaflets for a museum. The museum delivers 2,250 to hotels, 1,800 to restaurants and 2,750 to information centres.

How many leaflets are left over? _____

1 mark

PS 2. This table shows the number of people visiting a theme park during the six days it is open.

Day	Wednesday	Thursday	Friday	Saturday	Sunday	Monday
Adults	516	457	1,084	1,523	1,815	987
Children	369	388	843	1,056	1,634	865

How many more adults visited on the weekend than children? _____

1 mark

Challenge 2

PS 1. A stadium has a capacity of 75,932 people. A band stages two concerts in the stadium. All the tickets were sold for both concerts. 386 people did not attend the first concert and 1,084 did not attend the second concert.

How many people attended both concerts altogether? _____

1 mark

PS 2. This table shows the number of cars produced at two car factories.

Months in 2020	January	February	March	April	May	June
Factory 1	38,167	35,087	35,824	39,566	40,052	34,822
Factory 2	24,819	21,878	22,278	24,719	23,725	24,093

a) How many more cars were built in Factory 1 than in Factory 2 in February? _____

b) 3,208 more cars were built in Factory 2 in June 2020 than in June 2019.

How many cars were built in Factory 2 in June 2019?

_____

2 marks

Challenge 3

PS 1. A factory uses beads to make necklaces and bracelets.

There is a stock of 138,578 gold beads and 119,843 silver beads. 196,775 beads are used to make necklaces and bracelets.

How many beads are left? _____

1 mark

PS 2. This table shows the population of England, Scotland, Wales and Northern Ireland in 1950 and 2000.

Country	England	Scotland	Wales	N. Ireland
1950	38,668,830	5,095,969	2,596,850	1,370,921
2000	49,138,831	5,062,416	2,910,228	1,685,267

a) By how much more did the population of Northern Ireland increase than the population of Wales between 1950 and 2000?

_____

b) In 2000, how many people lived in England, Scotland, Wales and N. Ireland altogether?

_____

2 marks

Total: [ ] /8 marks

Had a go [ ]	**Getting there** [ ]	**Got it!** [ ]

Checking

- Use estimation to check answers to calculations
- Decide whether answers to problems are appropriate

Estimation

When calculating or solving word problems, it is good practice to find your answer using **estimation**. This can be done before the calculation. Then you can compare your actual answer with your estimation.

Example

46,547 + 32,007 + 45,618 =

Round each number to the nearest ten thousand to give a reasonable estimate:

50,000 + 30,000 + 50,000 = 130,000

This means that the actual answer to the calculation should be in the region of 130,000

```
    4  6  5  4  7
    3  2  0  0  7
+   4  5  6  1  8
────────────────────
1   2  4  1  7  2
    1  1     2
```

> As the actual answer is in the region of the estimated answer, it could be assumed to be correct.

It is also possible to check this answer by using an **inverse operation**.

Example

```
   0  ¹1 ¹3  6              4
   1  2  4 ¹1 1̶ ¹2    7  8  5  5̶ ¹4
−        4  5  6  1  8    3  2  0  0  7
────────────────────    ────────────────
         7  8  5  5  4    4  6  5  4  7
```

> The inverse operation works backwards from the answer giving the start number 46,547

Appropriate answers

When solving word problems, it is always important to make sure that the *question* is answered.

The answer to a calculation is not always the answer to the question.

Example

Joss is playing a computer game. Points are scored for silver and gold rings. He has 4,845 points for the silver rings and 5,177 points for the gold rings. Joss needs 10,000 points to get to the next level.

Has Joss scored enough points to move onto the next level?

> The answer to the question is 'Yes', although the answer to the calculation is (4,845 + 5,177 =) 10,022 or (10,022 − 10,000 =) 22

Tip

Make sure that you have answered the question in an appropriate way.

Remember

The answer to a *calculation* is not always the final answer to the *question* in a word problem.

Key words

- estimation
- inverse operation

Challenge 1

1. By rounding each number to the nearest thousand, give an estimated answer:

   a) 5,617 + 2,704 – 4,984 = _____

   b) 7,380 + 1,476 + 3,791 = _____

   c) 9,128 – 3,467 – 3,423 = _____

   3 marks

2. Write an inverse operation for these calculations.

   a) 53,872 + 23,782 = 77,654 _____

   b) 60,936 – 37,058 = 23,878 _____

   2 marks

PS 3. A container ship sails from New York to Liverpool carrying 7,826 containers. On the return journey it carries 6,902 containers.

   Tim works out the difference between the number of containers as 1,128 containers.

   Write an inverse calculation to show Tim has made a mistake.

   _____

   1 mark

Challenge 2

1. By rounding each number to the nearest ten thousand, give an estimated answer:

   a) 23,819 + 32,893 – 18,197 = _____

   b) 71,618 + 12,832 + 32,703 = _____

   c) 80,012 – 14,672 – 44,556 = _____

   3 marks

2. Write an inverse operation for this calculation.

   259,082 + 369,065 = 628,147 _____

   1 mark

PS 3. A factory bakes biscuits and puts them into boxes.

   In one hour, they bake 7,870 biscuits and they are put into boxes that hold 15 biscuits.

   How many boxes will be filled? _____

   1 mark

Challenge 3

1. By rounding each number to the nearest hundred thousand, give an estimated answer:

   a) 749,613 + 537,229 = _____

   b) 1,510,717 – 391,426 = _____

   c) 2,557,328 – 577,426 – 437,932 = _____

   3 marks

2. Complete the calculation and write an inverse operation for this calculation.

   590,769 + 1,219,362 = _____

   The inverse is _____

   2 marks

PS 3. Amol says, "I can write five 5-digit numbers that sum to 49,999."

   Explain why Amol is wrong. _____

   _____

   1 mark

Total: [ ] / 17 marks

Had a go [ ]   **Getting there** [ ]   **Got it!** [ ]

Special numbers and mental calculation

- Identify common factors, common multiples and prime numbers
- Perform mental calculations with mixed operations and larger numbers

Common multiples and common factors

Multiples are numbers that result from two whole numbers being multiplied.

Example

$4 \times 6 = 24$

24 is a multiple of 4 and 6

24 is a multiple of both 4 and 6, so it can be described as a **common multiple** of 4 and 6

Other common multiples of 4 and 6 would be 12, 36, 48, 60 and so on.

12 is the lowest number and so it is called the **lowest common multiple**.

Factors are whole numbers that are multiplied to get another whole number.

Example

$5 \times 12 = 60$

5 and 12 are factors of 60

$5 \times 15 = 75$

5 and 15 are factors of 75

5 is a factor of 60 and it is also a factor of 75, so 5 is a **common factor** of 60 and 75.

The common factors of 60 and 75 are 1, 3, 5, and 15

15 is the largest common factor and so is called the **highest common factor**.

> **Tip**
>
> Knowing number facts and multiplication and division facts can help you work out mental calculations.

Prime numbers

A **prime number** is a number greater than 1 that cannot be made by multiplying two whole numbers together, apart from multiplying by 1 and the number itself.

Example

To find prime numbers between 50 and 59, decide if the numbers can be divided by other whole numbers.

50   51   52   (53)   54   55   56   57   58   (59)

> 50, 52, 54, 56, 58 can be divided by 2
>
> 51, 54, 57 can be divided by 3
>
> 55 can be divided by 5
>
> So, **53 and 59 are the prime numbers**.

Mental calculations

Knowing number facts will help you when it comes to doing mental calculations.

- If you know $12 - 8 = 4$, you can work out that **1,200 − 800 = 400** and **12,000 − 8,000 = 4,000**
- If you know $30 \div 5 = 6$, you can work out that **3,000 ÷ 5 = 600** and **30,000 ÷ 50 = 600**

Use partitioning:

- $5{,}676 + 374 = \mathbf{5{,}000 + 600 + 70 + 6} + 300 + 70 + 4 = \mathbf{5{,}000 + 900 + 140 +}$ **10 = 6,050**
- $476 \times 4 = \mathbf{1{,}600} + 280 + 24 = \mathbf{1{,}904}$

Use factors:

- $\mathbf{350 \times 24} = 350 \times 6 \times 4 = 350 \times 6 \times 2 \times 2 = 2{,}100 \times 2 \times 2 = 4{,}200 \times 2 = \mathbf{8{,}400}$
- $\mathbf{6{,}400 \div 25} = 6{,}400 \div 100 \times 4 = 64 \times 4 = 64 \times 2 \times 2 = 128 \times 2 = \mathbf{256}$

> **Key words**
>
> - multiple
> - common multiple
> - lowest common multiple
> - factor
> - common factor
> - highest common factor
> - prime number

Challenge 1

1. Circle the multiples:

   a) **of 6**   14   34   48   56   72   84

   b) **of 9**   53   72   88   96   108   112

   2 marks

2. What is the highest common factor of 30 and 45? _____

   1 mark

3. Circle the number that is **not** a prime number.

       31   41   51   61   71

   1 mark

Challenge 2

1. Circle the multiples:

   a) **of 20**   110   150   160   300   350   420

   b) **of 25**   145   205   275   325   550   640

   2 marks

2. What is the lowest common multiple of:

   a) 5 and 6 _____

   b) 4 and 6 _____

   c) 4 and 12 _____

   3 marks

3. What is the highest common factor of:

   a) 24 and 36 _____

   b) 48 and 60 _____

   c) 30 and 65 _____

   3 marks

PS 4. Find three prime numbers that total 20 _____

   1 mark

Challenge 3

1. Common multiples of 6 and 15 are all multiples of which number? _____

   1 mark

2. What is the lowest common multiple of:

   a) 3 and 6 _____

   b) 12 and 15 _____

   c) 20 and 25 _____

   3 marks

3. What is the highest common factor of 26 and 78? _____

   1 mark

PS 4. Pam visits a supermarket every 3 days and Lily visits the supermarket every 5 days.

   If they both visit one Monday, what day will they next visit together?

   _____

   1 mark

PS 5. Find a 2-digit prime number which is still a prime number when the digits are reversed.

   _____

   1 mark

Total: [ ] /20 marks

| Had a go [ ] | Getting there [ ] | Got it! [ ] |

31

Written multiplication and division

- Multiply numbers with up to four digits by 2-digit numbers using long multiplication
- Divide numbers with up to four digits by 2-digit numbers using long and short division

Long multiplication

Long multiplication is a way of setting out a written multiplication.

Example

4,276 × 36

Step 1:
Set out.
Multiply by 6 first.

```
    4 2 7 6
×     3 6
  2 5 6 5 6
```

Step 2:
Multiply by 30
(This is × 10 × 3)
Record × 10 by writing 0

```
    4 2 7 6
×     3 6
  2 5 6 5 6
            0
```

Step 3:
Multiply by 3

```
      4 2 7 6
×       3 6
    2 5 6 5 6
+ 1 2 8 2 8 0
```

Step 4:
Add the two multiplications.

```
      4 2 7 6
×       3 6
    2 5 6 5 6
+ 1 2 8 2 8 0
  1 5 3 9 3 6
```

Short division

Short division is used when dividing by a 1-digit number or by a larger number you can confidently work out multiples for mentally. The calculations to find remainders are recorded in long division but are completed mentally for short division. It is best used only with numbers that allow for mental calculation easily.

Long division

Long division sets out the division showing all the working.

Example

3,675 ÷ 35 =

(Using multiples of 35 will help: 35 × 1 = 35, 35 × 2 = 70, 35 × 3 = 105, 35 × 4 = 140, 35 × 5 = 175 ...)

Step 1:
Set out.
3,600 ÷ 35 (= 100)
Subtract to find the remainder: 175

```
        1
3 5 3 6 7 5
  - 3 5 0 0
    1 7 5
```

Step 2:
Divide the remainder by 35
175 ÷ 35 = 5

```
        1 5
3 5 3 6 7 5
  - 3 5 0 0
    1 7 5
```

Step 3:
Calculate the remainder.
175 − (35 × 5) =
175 − 175 = 0

```
        1 5
3 5 3 6 7 5
  - 3 5 0 0
    1 7 5
    1 7 5
        0
```

Step 4:
Here a place holder 0 is needed.

```
      1 0 5
3 5 3 6 7 5
  - 3 5 0 0
    1 7 5
    1 7 5
        0
```

Tip

Try to remember carrying figures or write them elsewhere so they do not confuse the calculation.

Tip

Practising the routines of long multiplication and long division regularly will help you to calculate successfully.

Key words

- long multiplication
- short division
- long division

Work out your answers to these questions on a separate piece of paper if required.

Challenge 1

1. a) $67 \times 23 =$ _____

   b) $412 \times 16 =$ _____

   2 marks

2. a) $476 \div 4 =$ _____

   b) $575 \div 25 =$ _____

   2 marks

3. a) $552 \div 23 =$ _____

   b) $6,495 \div 15 =$ _____

   2 marks

PS 4. Keira multiplies 68 by 42. She estimates the answer will be about 2,800

   What is the difference between the actual answer and Keira's estimated answer? _____

   1 mark

Challenge 2

1. a) $254 \times 26 =$ _____

   b) $3,264 \times 19 =$ _____

   2 marks

2. a) $640 \div 40 =$ _____

   b) $7,575 \div 25 =$ _____

   2 marks

3. a) $3,438 \div 18 =$ _____

   b) $9,010 \div 85 =$ _____

   2 marks

PS 4. Harvey divides 5,270 by 25. Explain how you can tell that there will not be a whole number answer.

   _____

   _____

   1 mark

Challenge 3

1. a) $3,284 \times 16 =$ _____

   b) $4,746 \times 35 =$ _____

   c) $3,804 \times 48 =$ _____

   3 marks

2. a) $6,496 \div 32 =$ _____

   b) $6,900 \div 30 =$ _____

   c) $3,075 \div 15 =$ _____

   3 marks

3. a) $2,747 \div 41 =$ _____

   b) $7,784 \div 28 =$ _____

   c) $2,720 \div 85 =$ _____

   3 marks

PS 4. A number divided by 45 is 156 r 32. What was the number? _____

   1 mark

Total: ____ /24 marks

Had a go ☐   **Getting there** ☐   **Got it!** ☐

33

Problems and order of operations

- Solve problems involving addition, subtraction, multiplication and division
- Use knowledge of the order of operations to carry out calculations involving all four operations

Solve problems

You will come across problems that involve larger numbers and more steps.

Example

Sonya is making necklaces and bracelets with beads to sell at a market.

Each bracelet uses 45 beads and she makes 38 bracelets.

Each necklace uses 66 beads and she makes 54 necklaces.

She has a supply of 10,000 beads.

How many beads does she have left?

Solve this problem by breaking it up into smaller steps and thinking about facts that are needed.

1. How many beads are needed to make the bracelets?	2. How many beads are needed to make the necklaces?	3. How many beads are used altogether?	4. How many beads are left?

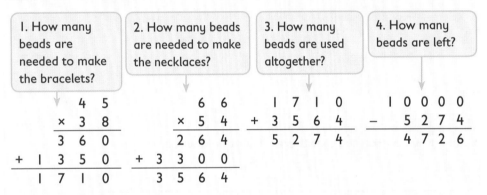

Answer: 4,726 beads are left

Order of operations

Some calculations use different operations. They need to be completed in a specific order.

To remember the order, use the abbreviation **BIDMAS**.

The operations must be completed in a specific order otherwise different incorrect answers may be found.

Example

$6 - 3 + 5 =$	Complete the calculations in order. (Completing the addition first will give a different and incorrect answer.)	$3 + 5 = 8$
$20 + 2 \times 5 =$	Complete the multiplication before the addition.	$20 + 10 = 30$
$30 - 5^2 =$	Complete the indices before the subtraction.	$30 - 25 = 5$
$(20 + 2) \times 5 =$	Complete the calculation in brackets first.	$22 \times 5 = 110$

Another abbreviation sometimes used is **BODMAS**. This is the same, but O stands for 'of' or multiplication, as in 5 lots of 4 = 20. Sometimes, it may stand for 'order' or 'order of operations'.

Remember

BIDMAS stands for:

Brackets — First, complete any calculation in brackets.

Indices — Second, calculate any indices (e.g. 3^2 or 2^3).

Division & **M**ultiplication — Third, calculate division and multiplication in the order they appear in the calculation.

Addition & **S**ubtraction — Fourth, calculate addition and subtraction in the order they appear in the calculation.

Key words

- BIDMAS
- BODMAS

Challenge 1

PS 1. A supermarket orders some trays of drinks. There are 48 small cans on a tray and 32 large cans on a tray. The supermarket orders 22 trays of small cans and 15 trays of large cans.

How many cans does the supermarket order altogether? _____

1 mark

PS 2. A company owns 9 cruise ships. Each ship can carry 1,368 passengers. Each cruise ship sails on 19 cruises a year.

What is the maximum number of passengers that could take a cruise in one year? _____

1 mark

3. a) $50 - 10 + 30 - 40 =$ [ ]

    b) $60 - 40 \div 2 =$ [ ]

    c) $80 + 10 \times 10 =$ [ ]

3 marks

Challenge 2

PS 1. There are 50 pencils in a box. A school orders 12 boxes of pencils.
There are 8 classes in the school; 3 of the classes have 29 children and the rest of the classes all have 28 children.

At the beginning of the school year, each child is given a new pencil.

How many pencils are left? _____

1 mark

PS 2. Find the missing number.

$562 \times 28 =$ _____ $\times 14$

1 mark

3. a) $75 \times (10 + 10) =$ [ ]

    b) $90 \div (45 - 15) =$ [ ]

    c) $200 - (50 + 10 - 5^2) =$ [ ]

3 marks

Challenge 3

PS 1. A rugby club holds 22 games at their ground in one season. The ground is full at 17 of these games. The rugby ground can hold 8,826 people. The crowds for four of the other games were 7,934; 8,244; 8,271 and 8,538.

Altogether, 191,045 people attend the 22 matches.
What was the crowd for the remaining game? _____

1 mark

2. a) $200 \times (100 \div 10) \times 2 =$ [ ]

    b) $1,000 \div 10 + 500 \times 10^2 =$ [ ]

    c) $500 - 240 \div (40 - 20) =$ [ ]

3 marks

3. Add brackets to these calculations to make them correct.

    a) $40 + 40 \times 20 + 20 = 3,200$
    b) $120 - 60 \times 2 + 120 \div 10 = 132$

2 marks

Total: [ ] / 16 marks

Had a go		Getting there		Got it!	

Progress test 2

1. Try to answer these calculations mentally or use an appropriate written method.

   a) $5,200 + 52,000 =$ _____

   b) $2,497 + 2,502 =$ _____

   c) $500 \times 30 =$ _____

   d) $8,000 \div 500 =$ _____

   e) $90,000 + 900 + 9 =$ _____

   f) $10,000 - 1 =$ _____

   6 marks

2. Write these numbers in order, starting with the smallest.

   3,734,189   3,876,210   3,732,767   3,876,034   3,876,155

   _____   _____   _____   _____   _____

   1 mark

3. Look at these number cards.

1	2	3	4	5	6

   Use each of these number cards once to make three 2-digit numbers that complete each statement.

   [ ][ ]   is a prime number.

   [ ][ ]   is a common multiple of 8 and 28.

   [ ][ ]   is a common factor of 64 and 96.

   3 marks

PS 4. Organisers arrange for 24,814 runners to take part in a fun-run.

   1,893 runners do not turn up on the day of the fun-run and 735 runners do not finish the run.

   How many runners did finish the fun-run? _____

   1 mark

5. Complete this table by rounding the numbers.

	Round to the nearest 10,000	Round to the nearest 1,000,000	Round to the nearest 50
4,925,193			
2,184,746			

   6 marks

6. Circle the number where the digit 4 has a value of forty thousand.

   1,405,391   2,730,540   3,854,056   40,357,129   5,841,986

   1 mark

7. $20 + 5 \times 4 - 4 =$ _____

   1 mark

PS 8. Carrie is skiing. She starts at the top of a mountain where the temperature is −7 °C. She skis down the mountain and sees that the temperature is 2 °C.

a) What is the difference in the two temperatures? _____

1 mark

b) At night, the temperature in the village falls 2 °C from 2 °C.

What is the temperature at night in the village? _____

1 mark

PS 9. Nisha must complete the following calculations. She works out an estimated answer by rounding.

a) 49,932 + 6,089 =

Nisha rounds both numbers to the nearest thousand.

What is Nisha's estimated answer? _____

1 mark

b) 5,670 ÷ 45 =

Nisha rounds 5,670 to the nearest thousand and 45 to the nearest 10.

What is Nisha's estimated answer? _____

1 mark

10. Write in numbers:

a) two million, three hundred and six thousand and fifty-one _____

b) five million, seventy-two thousand, four hundred and ten _____

2 marks

PS 11. Ned runs a chicken farm. One week his chickens lay 1,378 eggs. The eggs are put into boxes of 12. As many boxes as possible are filled.

How many boxes will be needed for all the eggs?

1 mark

12. Use long multiplication to calculate 6,847 × 74 =

1 mark

13. Use long division to calculate 2,448 ÷ 34 =

1 mark

PS 14. A concert is held in a stadium. Tickets are sold at the stadium and online.

5,562 tickets were sold at the stadium and 379 were sold at the stadium on the day of the concert.

19,803 tickets were sold online and 495 tickets were sold online on the day of the concert.

How many more tickets were sold online than sold at the stadium?

_____

1 mark

PS 15. A factory makes large and small teddy bears. The large teddy bears are packed into boxes of 18 teddy bears and the small teddy bears are packed into boxes of 32 teddy bears.

In one day, the factory fills 125 boxes of large teddy bears and 236 boxes of small teddy bears.

How many teddy bears are made altogether?

_____

1 mark

16. $12 - 20 + 6 =$ _____

1 mark

PS 17. A cruise ship has cabins for 3,275 passengers. There are 48 cabins for 4 people and 83 cabins for one person. The rest of the cabins are for two.

How many cabins for two people are there on the cruise ship?

_____

1 mark

18. What is the value of the digit 9 in this number?

6,952,781

_____

1 mark

19. $100,000 - 100 =$ [ ]

1 mark

PS 20. At the entrance to a harbour there are two lighthouses. The light of one lighthouse flashes every 18 seconds. The light of the second flashes every 20 seconds.

If the lights flash together, how long will it be before they flash together again? _____

1 mark

PS 21. A teacher is trying to organise a sports day. There are 246 children taking part. There must be fewer than 50 children in each team and there must be fewer than 12 teams. Each team must have an equal number of children.

How many teams will there be and how many children will be in each team?

_____ teams of _____ children

2 marks

PS 22. a) Find two different prime numbers that add to up 40 _____

b) Find three different prime numbers that add up to 40 _____

2 marks

23. Find the missing numbers in these calculations.

a)
```
      5 □ 6 3
    ×     □ 6
    ─────────
    3 2 7 7 8
  1 6 3 8 □ 0
  ───────────
  1 9 6 6 6 8
```

b)
```
      3 1 □ □
    ×     2 7
    ─────────
    2 2 1 6 □
  6 3 3 4 0
  ───────────
  8 5 5 0 9
```

2 marks

PS 24. When a new stadium was opened, two newspapers rounded the capacity of the stadium in different ways.

One newspaper rounded the capacity to the nearest hundred and reported it was 45,500

The other newspaper rounded the capacity to the nearest thousand and reported it was 45,000

What could the smallest actual capacity be? _____

1 mark

25. Write in words: 5,040,300

_____

1 mark

26. Add a pair of brackets to each calculation to make them correct.

a) $80 - 60 \times 40 + 20 = 820$

b) $300 \div 30 + 30 - 50 = 30$

Add two pairs of brackets to each calculation to make them correct.

c) $100 - 5^2 \times 100 - 90 = 750$

d) $10^2 \div 40 + 10 \times 10^2 - 90 = 20$

4 marks

PS 27. Ayesha and her friends have made cupcakes for a fair. She places 16 cupcakes onto a full tray. There are 32 full trays and there are 12 cupcakes on the final tray.

They sell 488 cupcakes.

How many trays will they need for the unsold cupcakes? _____

1 mark

PS 28. Find the missing numbers.

a) [ ] $\div 28 = 98$

b) [ ] $\div 18 = 265$

c) [ ] $\div 37 = 86 \text{ r } 23$

3 marks

Total: [ ] /51 marks

39

Similar sounding word endings I

- Distinguish between words that are often confused
- Learn to spell tricky words

Confusing spellings

The **word endings** -**ant** and -**ent**, -**ance** and -**ence**, and -**ancy** and -**ency** are easy to confuse and misspell. For many of these words, there is no guidance to follow; they just have to be learned. There are some, however, where simple rules can be helpful.

It is also useful to know other words in the **word family**, as it is likely that they will follow the same spelling pattern.

<table><tr><td>

Remember

If you are unsure of the correct spelling of a word ending, refer to a dictionary for help.
</td></tr></table>

Words ending -ant, -ance and -ancy

Often, the word endings -**ant**, -**ance**/-**ancy** will have a related word which also uses an **a** in the suffix.

Example

observation has an **a** in the word ending, thus **observant** and **observance**.

- They were very observ**ant**.
- There was good observ**ance** of the rules.

tolerate/toleration both have the **a** in the word ending, thus **tolerant** and **tolerance**.

- They were toler**ant** of each other.
- They showed toler**ance** to the heat.

hesitate/hesitation both have the **a** in the word ending, thus **hesitant** and **hesitance**.

- They were hesit**ant** about crossing the road.
- There was a moment's hesit**ance** before they crossed the road.
- Their hesit**ancy** saved their lives as a car sped around the corner.

substantial, **substantive** and **substance** all have a similar spelling pattern.

- The events had several witnesses so their story had some subst**ance**.

> **Tip**
>
> Look out for words with these endings. Keep in mind that there are many exceptions to be aware of.

Words ending -ent, -ence and -ency

The word endings -**ent**, -**ence**/-**ency** often follow a soft **c** sound, soft **g** sound or **qu**.

Example

innocent ⇨ innoc**ence**   *The judge declared him innoc**ent**.*
*The judge was convinced of his innoc**ence**.*

agent ⇨ ag**ency**   *She wanted to become a travel ag**ent**.*
*The ag**ency** was doing very well.*

frequent ⇨ frequ**ency**   *The buses needed to be more frequ**ent**.*
*The buses now run with greater frequ**ency**.*

Always consider the word family or the **root word** (spelling and meaning) when adding word endings.

> **Key words**
>
> - word ending
> - word family
> - root word

Challenge 1

1. Rewrite each word with the correct **-ant** or **-ent** ending.

   a) tolerate _____

   b) confidence _____

   c) expect _____

   d) assist _____

   e) contest _____

   f) patience _____

Challenge 2

1. Change each of the words below to an **-ancy** or **-ency** ending and use it in a sentence. Use a dictionary to help you, if you need to.

   a) urgent

   _____

   b) vacant

   _____

   c) pregnant

   _____

   d) consistent

   _____

Challenge 3

1. Change each of the words below to an **-ancy** or **-ency** ending and use it in a sentence. Use a dictionary to help you, if you need to.

   a) fluent

   _____

   b) resident

   _____

   c) redundant

   _____

   d) buoyant

   _____

2. Complete each sentence with the most suitable form of the words below.

   confide　　**contest**　　**innocent**　　**ignore**　　**triumph**　　**consult**

   a) The woman proved her _____ to the police.

   b) They showed great _____ by not following the rules.

   c) He showed a lot of _____ as he climbed the rock face.

   d) He was the only _____ to turn up at the competition.

   e) She has to see the _____ at the hospital next week.

   f) They were _____ because their plan had worked so well.

Total: ☐ /20 marks

Had a go ☐　　**Getting there** ☐　　**Got it!** ☐

Similar sounding word endings 2

- Distinguish between words that are often confused
- Learn to spell tricky words

Confusing spellings

The **word endings -able**, **-ible**, **-ably** and **-ibly** are easy to confuse and misspell. It is worth remembering that -able/-ably are far more common so can be used as a 'best bet' if you are unsure.

The word endings -able and -ably are generally used if there is a related word ending in **-ation**. They are also often used if the complete **root word** can be heard or seen, but there are exceptions.

Example

apply ⇨ applic**able** or applic**ably**

> **application** is in the same **word family**, so these words are related.

break ⇨ break**able**
like ⇨ like**able**

> The root words 'break' and 'like' can still be heard in full when the word ending is added.

For words ending in **ce** or **ge**, the **e** remains when **-able** or **-ably** is added. Retaining the 'e' keeps the c and the g sounds 'soft'.

The word endings **-ible** and **-ibly** are added when only part of the word can be heard. But note that there are exceptions to this rule, e.g. sens**ible** where the complete word 'sense' *can* be heard.

Example

poss**ible** ⇨ poss**ibly**
vis**ible** ⇨ vis**ibly**

> **poss** and **vis** come from Latin and only become full words in English when a suffix is added.

Letter string 'ough'

Words that contain the letter string **ough** are often confusing as **ough** represents different sounds in different words. Words with the **ough** spelling pattern just have to be learnt.

Example

b**ough**t   r**ough**   th**ough**   thr**ough**
thor**ough**   pl**ough**   c**ough**

> **ough** makes a different sound in each of these words.

Adding suffixes to words ending -fer

If the **-fer** ending of a word is still stressed when a suffix is added, the **r** is **doubled** before adding the **suffix**. If the **-fer** ending is *not* stressed in the new word, then **r** is *not* doubled.

Example

refer ⇨ refer**r**al
prefer ⇨ prefer**r**ing

> The **-fer** part of refer and prefer is stressed when spoken; the stress remains after the suffix is added so the **r** is doubled.

prefer ⇨ prefer**ence**
transfer ⇨ transfer**ence**

> **-fer** is not stressed after the suffix **-ence** is added, so the **r** is *not* doubled.

Challenge 1

1. Rewrite each word correctly with the given ending. Remember that in some cases, the spelling might change slightly.

   a) prefer + ed _____

   b) differ + ence _____

   c) transfer + ing _____

   d) refer + ing _____

   e) refer + ee _____

   f) prefer + ing _____

6 marks

Challenge 2

1. Use each of the given words correctly in a sentence.

   a) though

   _____

   _____

   b) through

   _____

   _____

   c) thorough

   _____

   _____

   d) bought

   _____

   _____

   e) brought

   _____

   _____

5 marks

Challenge 3

1. Complete each sentence with the most suitable ending from **-able**, **-ably**, **-ible** and **-ibly**.

   a) The test was **unquestion**_____ harder this year.

   b) One hundred is **divis**_____ by ten.

   c) She was **poss**_____ the greatest singer ever heard.

   d) The school rules were **applic**_____ to everybody.

   e) They were **terr**_____ sorry for the trouble they had caused.

   f) The children were **uncontroll**_____ when the food came out.

6 marks

Total: ____ / 17 marks

Had a go ☐   **Getting there** ☐   **Got it!** ☐

Spellings: 'ei' and 'ie'

- Recognise where the i before e 'rule' is applicable

The 'ei' spelling

The letters **'ei'** in words can often make the sound represented by **ee** in p**ee**p.

Example

ceiling

receive

seize

These words all contain **ei** which make the **ee** sound.

Remember

ei can make the ee sound represented by ee in 'peep' but it can also make other sounds, e.g. in 'beige', 'height' and 'foreign'.

The rule: i before e except after c

A well-known 'spelling rule' is that **i** comes before **e** in spelling unless it follows the letter **c**, in which case **ei** is used.

Example

relief

priest

shriek

These words follow the 'i before e except after c' rule.

receive

deceive

These words also follow the rule: the **ei** follows the letter **c**.

It is important to note that the **ei** in both words is making the **ee** sound as in 'peep'.

Although many words follow this rule, in fact, there are a lot of exceptions to the rule as well. Some words use **ei**, even when the letters do *not* follow a **c**. Many other words have **i** before **e**, even after a **c**.

Tip

If unsure whether to use **ei** or **ie**, think about whether the two letters are making an **ee** sound. If so, the best bet is to use **ie**.

Example

protein

seize

caffeine

These words are just three of many. In these words **ei** makes the **ee** sound but does not follow a **c**.

science

efficient

In these words **ie** is used but *does* follow a **c**.

It is important to remember that with these two words, the **ie** does not make that **ee** sound as in 'p**ee**p'.

The **ei** and **ie** letters often make the **ee** sound (as in 'peep') but in some words, they make other sounds.

Example

friend

height

foreign

These words use **ie** and **ei** to make different sounds to 'ee'.

Challenge I

1. Add **ei** or **ie** to give each word its correct spelling. Then circle all words in which **ei** or **ie** make the long **ee** sound.

ch_ _f   c_ _ling   h_ _ght   p_ _ce   v_ _n   r_ _ndeer

b_ _ge   n_ _ghbour   dec_ _ve   th_ _f   w_ _ght   misch_ _f

18 marks

Challenge 2

1. a) Place a tick next to each word that is spelt correctly. Use a dictionary to help you if needed.

recieve ☐

believe ☐

conceive ☐

deciet ☐

perceive ☐

seize ☐

protien ☐

cieling ☐

b) Write out correctly any words that were spelt incorrectly in part a).

_____

_____

8 marks

Challenge 3

1. a) Think about the words **field** and **receipt**. Complete the 'rule' below.

i comes before **e** except after **c** if the **ie/ei** makes _____

_____

_____

b) Write a sentence using each of the words given in part a).

_____

_____

_____

_____

3 marks

Total: ☐ /29 marks

Had a go ☐   **Getting there** ☐   **Got it!** ☐

Homophones and near-homophones

- Recognise homophones and near-homophones

Homophones

Words that sound the same but have different spellings and meanings are known as **homophones**. It is important to know the difference between these words to avoid confusion when reading and writing; using the wrong word will change the meaning of what you are trying to say.

Example

- **profit** and **prophet**
  - A **profit** was made selling cakes at playtime.
  - A **prophet** told them what the future would hold.
- **license** and **licence**
  - His job is to **license** buses for use in the city.
  - She has a driving **licence**.
- **morning** and **mourning**
  - It was a beautiful **morning**.
  - They were **mourning** the death of their elderly aunt.
- **complement** and **compliment**
  - He had a red tie to **complement** his posh suit.
  - It was a nice **compliment** to be praised at school.

Near-homophones

Some words cause confusion by sounding similar but not quite the same. These words are known as **near-homophones**. They have similar spellings, but different meanings.

Example

- **device** (noun) and **devise** (a verb)
  - They had a special **device** for checking the speed of the bike.
  - They needed to **devise** a plan for their day out.
- **desert** (noun), **desert** (verb) and **dessert** (noun)
  - The camels walked across the hot **desert**.
  - I am scared that she is going to **desert** me.
  - I'd like ice-cream for **dessert**.

> **Remember**
>
> There may only be a very slight difference in spelling between homophones but the meaning can be quite different.

> **Tip**
>
> Think about the context of the text and use a dictionary if you are still unsure.

> Pronounced with the emphasis on the first syllable. It means *open, sandy expanses*.

> Pronounced with the emphasis on the second syllable. It means *to abandon*.

> Pronounced the same as the verb 'desert', with the emphasis on the second syllable. It means *sweet course/pudding*.

> **Key words**
>
> - homophones
> - near-homophones
> - noun
> - verb

1. Underline the correct homophone in each sentence.

   a) I didn't know **weather / whether** the film would be any good or not.

   b) It was raining earlier; it was **pouring / poring** down.

   c) We **led / lead** the way on our bikes.

   d) The flag pole was made from **steal / steel**.

   4 marks

1. Look at the underlined words. Write the correct homophone or near-homophone for each.

   a) Lena wanted a **break / brake** from her homework. _____

   b) The school clothes sale made a good profit to the **sum / some** of £200. _____

   c) James **past / passed** his driving test yesterday. _____

   d) He **practiced / practised** his guitar every single day. _____

   4 marks

1. Write a sentence for each homophone. Use a dictionary to help you.

   a) principal

   _____

   b) principle

   _____

   2 marks

2. Write a sentence for each homophone. Use a dictionary to help you.

   a) rode

   _____

   b) rowed

   _____

   2 marks

3. Write a sentence for each near-homophone. Use a dictionary to help you.

   a) accept

   _____

   b) except

   _____

   2 marks

4. Write a sentence for each near-homophone. Use a dictionary to help you.

   a) advice

   _____

   b) advise

   _____

   2 marks

Total: ____ / 16 marks

Had a go ☐ **Getting there** ☐ **Got it!** ☐

47

Using a dictionary and thesaurus

- Use a dictionary to check the spelling and meaning of words
- Use a thesaurus to find synonyms of words

Using a dictionary

Dictionaries are essential for looking up words when you are both reading and writing. You can use a dictionary to check the spelling of words, particularly if you already know most of the spelling. You can also use a dictionary to check the **definition** of the word to make sure it is the correct word to use.

Example

If you are unsure whether the correct spelling is receipt or reciept, and whether it fits with what is being written, use the first three letters to locate the word in the dictionary.
The correct spelling can then be found.

receed

receipt

receive

recent

> Knowing the first few letters of a word makes it easier to find the word in the dictionary.

The definition is also given:

noun   proof that something has been received
She paid and was given a **receipt**.

> The definition states that the word receipt is a noun, explains what it means and gives an example of its use in a sentence.

Using a thesaurus

A **thesaurus** provides **synonyms** of words. It is used to help find a more suitable or more interesting word of similar meaning. A thesaurus will also often provide antonyms – words with an opposite meaning to the focus word.

Words in a thesaurus are usually ordered alphabetically as in a dictionary. Once a word has been located, you will see a list of synonyms.

Example

smart
adj   intelligent – brainy, bright, sharp
adj   stylish – dashing, fine, spruce
verb   hurt – ache, throb, sting

The above example provides synonyms for the word **smart**. It gives three different meanings (**intelligent**, **stylish** and **hurt**) two of which are adjectives and one that is a verb. Each meaning then has three synonyms which could be used to replace 'smart' in a sentence, depending on the context.

Care must be taken when selecting synonyms. Always check that the synonym used conveys the same meaning as the original word.

Challenge 1

1. Use a dictionary to find the word class of each word.

    a) happy   _____

    b) table   _____

    c) she   _____

    3 marks

2. Use a dictionary to find the different word classes of each word.

    a) steal   _____ and _____

    b) steel   _____ and _____

    2 marks

Challenge 2

1. Write a dictionary definition for each word below.

    complement   _____

    _____

    compliment   _____

    _____

    prophecy   _____

    _____

    prophesy   _____

    _____

    wary   _____

    _____

    weary   _____

    _____

    6 marks

Challenge 3

1. Use a thesaurus to find three synonyms for each word.

    deceive   _____   _____   _____

    receive   _____   _____   _____

    seize   _____   _____   _____

    9 marks

2. Read the text below. For each underlined word, choose a synonym which fits with the text.

    > You can see **many** **big** cranes, each one changing the city day-by-day as new **buildings** **grow** skywards.

    many   _____

    big   _____

    buildings _____

    grow   _____

    4 marks

    Total: ☐ **/24 marks**

Had a go ☐	Getting there ☐	Got it! ☐

Morphology and etymology

- **Use knowledge of morphology and etymology in spelling**

Morphology

The **morphology** of a word refers to the way it is made up from a **root word** and any **prefixes** or **suffixes**.

Example

The words **boy** and **boys** have the same morphology and only slightly different meanings.

The same morphology can also be used to create entirely new words such as **boyish** or **boyhood**.

The words **boy**, **boys**, **boyish** and **boyhood** all belong to the same **word family**.

Etymology

Etymology is concerned with a word's history – its origins. Many words in English originated in the Greek, Latin and French languages.

Example

Latin origins

Conscious (meaning 'aware and knowing what is going on around you') and **conscience** (meaning 'knowing what is right and wrong') both originate from **con-** + **scio**, which in Latin mean **with** (*con*) and **I know** (*scio*). This is, of course, where the word **science** also originates from.

Other words of Latin origin include:

Latin word	Meaning	English word
amio	*I love*	**amiable**
corpus	*body*	**corpse**
manus	*hand*	**manual**
moveo	*I move*	**movement**
tempus	*time*	**temporary**

Greek origins

Words of Greek origin include:

Greek word	Meaning	English word
pathos	suffer	**pathetic**
bios	life	**biology**
aster	star	**astrology**
logos	speech	**dialogue**

French origins

Many **ch** words (e.g. **ch**ef, ma**ch**ine, bro**ch**ure, para**ch**ute) originate from French. Many words ending in **-gue** and **-que** (e.g. vague, colleague, antique, unique) also originate from French.

Recognising word origins and word families helps when trying to use or spell words, as connections can be made with other familiar words.

1. The following prefixes have Latin origins. Draw lines to join each prefix with its meaning and the English word that derives from it.

Latin	Meaning	Word
prim-	out	aquarium
ex-	hearing	primary
audi-	first	expel
aqua-	water	auditory

4 marks

1. Write a sentence containing each given word of French origin.

    a) machine _____

    _____

    b) chandelier _____

    _____

    c) unique _____

    _____

    d) vague _____

    _____

4 marks

1. Look at the list of prefixes and other words of Greek origin. Use each one to form two English words that are used today.

    a) grapho (I write) _____ _____

    b) micro- (small) _____ _____

    c) tele- (from afar) _____ _____

    d) skopeo (I see) _____ _____

    e) photo- (light) _____ _____

10 marks

2. Select one word you have formed for each prefix above and write a sentence containing that word.

    a) _____

    _____

    b) _____

    _____

    c) _____

    _____

    d) _____

    _____

    e) _____

    _____

5 marks

Total: ☐ /23 marks

Had a go ☐   **Getting there** ☐   **Got it!** ☐

Organising and presenting non-fiction texts

- Use organisational and presentational devices to structure text and guide the reader

Non-fiction texts

The purpose of **non-fiction** texts is to share information with the reader. There are many different types of non-fiction texts, e.g. recount, information text, persuasive text, newspaper report, instructions.

There are many ways to organise and present non-fiction texts in order to share the information clearly and logically. Often it is useful to use a variety of different features.

Writing features and devices for non-fiction

Subheadings – Used to organise the text logically into different sections and help the reader to locate the information more easily. In a newspaper report, these are sometimes mini-headlines or just one or two-word summaries of a piece of interesting information from a section of text.

Illustrations – Pictures, diagrams, graphs and tables are useful because they can present information concisely – only a few words are needed and the picture says the rest.

Bullet points – Some of the information may be presented in an easy-to-read list using **bullet points**. These might include:

- key words
- important dates
- information about key events or ideas

Fact boxes – Fact boxes contain information linked to the main text but not key information. They add further interest for the reader.

Emphasising text – Words or phrases in the text can be highlighted in bold, underlined or written in a different colour or font, indicating important information or key facts. Sometimes these words are used to make up a glossary.

Emotional language – A common feature of persuasive texts where the reader is being addressed directly. It is used to make the reader consider the impact of what they are being persuaded about, e.g. *If you do not vote for Emily Fox, there will be nobody in the Child Interests group to defend your right to play areas and safe spaces – you will have a reduced quality of life.*

Rhetorical questions – Also common in persuasive texts but can also be used in other texts. A **rhetorical question** is not used to test the reader but to either make them realise they did not know something (e.g. *Did you know that there are over 1,000 species of sharks?*) or to make them think about a situation (e.g. *What would happen if everybody threw their litter on the ground?*).

Quotations – Sometimes, a person is quoted in the text. In a newspaper report, this may be a witness to an event, e.g. *Jack Brown, 14, from Bridgeville told us, 'There was a big fireball in the sky. I saw it pass over the town and then crash in the woods behind the park. There was a loud bang.'*

In a persuasive text, a quote might be used to support a point being made, e.g. *Highly respected town mayor, Charlie Redwood, has constantly told the Council that, 'Only Emily Fox will protect the rights of children. She must be voted for to protect childhood in our town.'*

Challenge I

1. Read the text and then put the key information into three bullet points.

> Mo Farah is a winner. He has won many gold medals over the 5,000m and 10,000m distances including five in European Championships, six in World Championships and four in the Olympic Games.

Mo's Golden Haul:

- _____
- _____
- _____

3 marks

Challenge 2

1. Read the persuasive letter below.

> Dear Residents,
>
> You represent all that is good about our wonderful village. Whether new or longstanding habitants, it is you who makes this such a fantastic place to live.
>
> I know many of you have been 'promised financial reward' by Tuckers Construction to agree to a new factory – which will be dirty, noisy, smelly and polluting – being built on the edge of your village.
>
> Tuckers Construction must not be allowed to build this. Do you really think they will give us money once we have agreed? Our highly respected local Countryside Ranger, Jeff Thomas, yesterday told the Council meeting, 'Tuckers Construction are irresponsible. They have no respect for the environment and even less for residents.' Is this what we want in Hillsworth?
>
> I am sure you will agree that this village stands for fairness, compassion and community – your community, our community. I urge you to protect it for the sake of ourselves and future generations.
>
> Yours in anticipation of keeping our village proud, safe and happy,
>
> Isabelle Trechard

a) How does the first paragraph involve the reader in the content of the letter?

_____

b) There are two questions in the text. What type of question are they and why are they used?

_____
_____

2 marks

Challenge 3

a) Read paragraphs two and three of the letter in Challenge 2. Find and copy three words or phrases that suggest that the company and construction will be a bad thing for the village.

_____
_____
_____

b) How does the quote from Jeff Thomas, and its introduction, support the argument?

_____
_____

4 marks

Total: [ ] /9 marks

Had a go [ ]   **Getting there** [ ]   **Got it!** [ ]

Developing settings and characters in fiction texts

- Produce effective descriptions of settings and characters
- Integrate dialogue into descriptions of settings and characters

Enhancing description

When producing effective descriptions of characters and settings in writing, the use of high-quality **noun phrases**, **adverbs**, **adjectives** and **figurative language** all play their part.

Adding **dialogue** can also help to give more information about what is happening in the story.

Example

Read the two versions of the same story opening.

> The dark waters flowed rapidly. Si found it hard to stay afloat, never mind swim. It would be tough enough without the thick clothes even in daylight. Hal struggled to keep the torchlight on him from the violently bobbing boat. On one occasion, he disappeared beneath the surface. It was terrifying. When he reappeared, Hal managed to grab his shoulder and haul his older brother into the boat.

> The dark waters flowed rapidly.
>
> "I'm not going to make it," shouted Si, the weight of his thick clothing and the swirling water pushing at him and dragging him down. Hal struggled to keep the torchlight on him.
>
> "The sea is too rough. I can't keep the torch on you," yelled Hal.
>
> "I can't …" Si's terrified words were cut short as he disappeared beneath the surface.
>
> As he reappeared, Hal grabbed him and hauled him aboard.
>
> "I got you buddy, I got you," he sobbed, relieved after fearing he would never see his older brother again.

In the first example, the setting (a river) is introduced along with two characters, Si (who is clearly having trouble in the water) and Hal who rescues him. There is lots of action and it seems like an interesting story opening.

In the second example, the setting and characters are introduced in a very similar way but more information and feeling is added through spoken words, and some of the description is given through speech too. Rather than the sentence about the violently bobbing boat, Hal's words are used to help describe the setting – "The sea is too rough."

Danger is emphasised through Si's words, "I'm not going to make it." and "I can't …". The phrases show how the words are spoken and also add to the description – 'Si's terrified words were cut short'. Similarly, Hal's sobbed words give away how relieved he is and that at least part of this relief is down to them being brothers.

Remember

Using a range of descriptive vocabulary helps the reader to imagine characters, settings and events.

Key words

- noun phrase
- adverb
- adjective
- figurative language
- dialogue

1. Draw lines to match the dialogue to the descriptions below.

a)
> "I can't breathe," she gasped.
> "Crawl under it," he yelled, "I can see the door."

b)
> "Keep pedalling," encouraged the coach from the car. "One more mile and you've won."

c)
> "Just delightful," she said. "Everything about this deserves to win. What a talent."

1
> He was approaching the last mile. Shouts of support told him he was going to win.

2
> The judge looked at and commented on it. She was clearly impressed and smiled.

3
> The thick acrid smoke filled the room and attacked their lungs. They dropped to the floor.

3 marks

Challenge 2

1. Look at the two pieces of text about cycling in Challenge 1.

Explain what additional information is given in the piece containing dialogue.

_____

_____

2 marks

2. Read the setting description below, then rewrite the second to fourth sentences using dialogue.

> Joe and Eve were deep in the forest. They struggled to walk through the thick, thorny undergrowth. Vines tangled around their feet. It was becoming too dark to see.

_____

_____

_____

_____

_____

3 marks

Challenge 3

1. Describe two people on a fairground ride, including dialogue. You might want to use words such as 'squealed', 'laughed' and 'screamed'.

_____

_____

_____

_____

_____

_____

_____

3 marks

Total: [　] / 11 marks

Had a go [　]　　**Getting there** [　]　　**Got it!** [　]

Cohesive devices

- Build cohesion between sentences and paragraphs in your writing

Building cohesion

Cohesion between sentences and paragraphs makes writing flow better and therefore more enjoyable to read.

Cohesion can be achieved by including **time connectives** (e.g. then, next, at first, afterwards), **conjunctions** (e.g. because, so, when, and), **adverbs** (e.g. suddenly, quickly, carefully), and **adverbial phrases** ('as fast as possible', 'before they had lunch') in your writing.

> **Remember**
>
> The better the writing, the more engaged the reader will be.

Example

Read these two versions of part of a story.

> Lucy crept into the room. It was dark and there was a musty, old smell. The door creaked behind her. She turned around to look. It slammed shut. She felt a cool breeze. It went very cold. A blue glowing frost allowed her to see the shapes of the wooden furniture it covered.

> Slowly, Lucy crept into the room. As she did so, she noticed the old, musty smell from within the darkness. The door creaked. Quickly turning round, she saw it slam shut. She felt a cool breeze. Suddenly, it became freezing cold and a blue glowing frost appeared, illuminating the shapes of the wooden furniture it covered.

In the first example the sentences are little more than a list of events. The sequence is fine and there is some good description, but further cohesion can be added.

In the second example, cohesion is much improved with the addition of the words and phrases in green. These show how and when things were happening and link the sentences more clearly and effectively.

Ellipsis for cohesion

The three dots of the **ellipsis** are useful for cohesion. The ellipsis can be used to show unfinished ideas, or a pause, to give the reader time for thought and in that way lead into the next part of the text. Even more dramatically, the ellipsis can be used to increase tension.

Example

> Lucy stared at the ice, as it now crawled along the floor and up the walls. Then she saw it...

> She now froze herself. She tried to scream but no sound would come out. It started to move towards her...

> **Key words**
>
> - cohesion
> - time connective
> - conjunction
> - adverb
> - adverbial phrase
> - ellipsis

In the above example, the ellipsis at the end of each paragraph creates tension but also provides cohesion with the words that come next, through the reader's anticipation of the content.

Challenge 1

1. a) Which set of sentences has the best cohesion? Tick one.

A
> The car went fast. It went over the bridge. The car turned the bend. It went through a hedge, surprisingly. It crashed into the river.

B
> Racing along, the car crossed over the bridge before turning the bend. Without warning, it then crashed through a hedge and plunged into the river.

☐   ☐   ☐

1 mark

b) Explain your choice above, making reference to some of the words used to improve cohesion.

_____

_____

_____

2 marks

Challenge 2

1. Read the text.

> Carefully, they inched along the narrow path, not daring to look down. AJ did not notice the small crack in the dusty path. As her foot touched it, she felt the loose earth give way a little. Before she had chance to react, the ground gave way.
>
> It took several moments before she realised the safety line had saved her.

Where do you think an ellipsis could be placed in this text? Explain your answer.

_____

_____

_____

2 marks

Challenge 3

1. Rewrite the extract below to make it more cohesive. Try to include at least four cohesive devices.

> All the way home from football practice, Noah cried. He was upset. He didn't score a goal today. His mum said it wasn't all about scoring goals. To Noah it was. At home his mum gave him some chocolate to cheer him up. He loved chocolate. He was happy. He went into the garden to practise scoring goals.

_____

_____

_____

_____

_____

_____

_____

_____

4 marks

Total: ☐ /9 marks

Had a go ☐   **Getting there** ☐   **Got it!** ☐

Précis

- Be able to précis longer passages

What is précis?

Précis is the skill of **summarising** the key information in a longer piece of writing to make it shorter. It is useful to be able to do this, especially when making notes or trying to explain the key points from more detailed information.

There are a number of ways to précis a passage of text:

- By generalising the text
- By removing unnecessary text
- By removing longer descriptions
- By changing longer phrases into shorter/simpler ones

Example

Précis by generalising the text

The lions, hungry and thirsty, make their way across the dry grasslands. Their prey is at least two days ahead and itself struggling to survive. Unless they can catch up, the lions will not live more than another week or so.

⇩

The lions are hungry and thirsty and need to catch up with their prey or they will die.

Précis by removing unnecessary text

Henry VIII had a vast appetite, which he fuelled with deer, wild boar, various game birds and any other meat he could get his hands on, caught while out hunting. Incredible amounts of food were served over several courses, brought to tables by servants over long evenings of eating at sumptuous banquets.

⇩

Henry VIII had a vast appetite, which he fuelled with huge amounts of meat, caught while out hunting. Incredible amounts of food were served at long, sumptuous banquets.

Précis by removing longer descriptions

Luxurious bedrooms and wide, sweeping open spaces displaying fine art make this hotel special. It is like a royal palace, and the food served in the exquisite restaurant is fit for royalty.

⇩

It is a luxurious hotel, fit for royalty.

Précis by changing longer phrases into shorter/simpler ones

They decided to go back to the drawing board with their plans.

⇩

They started again.

When writing description, **figurative language** and creating imagery for the reader is important. When précising a text, the opposite is true. A précis needs to summarise the key information.

Read the passage below and use it to answer the Challenges.

Wimbledon is the oldest and most famous tennis tournament in the world. It is played at the end of June each year at the prestigious All England Tennis Club in Wimbledon, London. The best tennis players compete on grass courts over two weeks for the honour of being crowned male or female champion. In addition to that honour, the women's and men's singles champions each win over £2 million. On top of that, they will receive even greater sums from sponsors keen to use their name and image to promote their products.

Challenge 1

1. Find and copy the key words or phrases from the passage to answer each question below.

    a) What? _____

    _____

    b) Where? _____

    _____

    c) When? _____

    _____

    3 marks

Challenge 2

1. Précis the passage, making sure you cover all the main points.

    _____

    _____

    _____

    _____

    _____

    _____

    _____

    4 marks

Challenge 3

1. Précis a short non-fiction text or a story that you have read.

    _____

    _____

    _____

    _____

    _____

    _____

    _____

    1 mark

Total: [ ] /8 marks

Had a go [ ]   **Getting there** [ ]   **Got it!** [ ]

Progress test 3

1. Write an antonym for the underlined word in each sentence.

   a) I am feeling **nervous** about the maths test next week. _____

   b) When the alarm went off at 6am, I felt really **energetic**. _____

   c) It was a **straightforward** drive to Sara's house. _____

   d) He **accepted** my help. _____

   e) My parents **punished** me for my behaviour at school. _____

   f) It was a very **powerful** speech. _____

2. Rewrite each word correctly with the given ending.

   a) transfer + ence   _____

   b) defer + al   _____

   c) suffer + ing   _____

   d) confer + ence   _____

   e) prefer + ing   _____

3. Underline the correct homophone in each sentence.

   a) The drinks were on the middle **aisle / isle** in the shop.

   b) The **bridal / bridle** shop was having a half price sale.

   c) The dog **beared / bared** its teeth.

   d) The vehicle was **stationery / stationary** when the bus hit it.

   e) The **whether / weather** forecast was not looking promising for our picnic.

   f) Yesterday we **rowed / rode** our horses over the moor.

4. Read the text and then write the key information for Janey's jobs as bullet points.

   > Janey realised she had lots of jobs to do. There was her homework, packing her PE bag and she also had to feed the cat. Her mum had also asked her to hang out the washing, clean the kitchen and tidy her bedroom.

   _____

   _____

   _____

   _____

   _____

   _____

   _____

   _____

5. Underneath each picture, write a sentence containing onomatopoeia to fit with the image.

a)

b)

c)

_____   _____   _____
_____   _____   _____
_____   _____   _____
_____   _____   _____
_____   _____   _____

6. Use each of the given words correctly in a sentence.

a) observant _____
_____

b) hesitant _____
_____

c) obedient _____
_____

d) substance _____
_____

7. Use a thesaurus to find three synonyms for each word.

a) thorough _____   _____   _____
b) thought _____   _____   _____
c) rough _____   _____   _____

8. Write a dictionary definition for each word below.

a) led _____
_____

b) lead _____
_____

c) desert _____
_____

d) dessert _____
_____

e) mourning _____

_____

f) morning _____

_____

6 marks

9. **Describe two people in a spooky house. Include dialogue to give more information about the characters and setting.**

_____

_____

_____

_____

_____

_____

_____

_____

_____

_____

_____

_____

_____

3 marks

10. **Read the two text extracts below.**

A

She placed the dish on the floor. Her eyes kept looking at the wolf's eyes. She stepped slowly, softly. She closed the gate of the enclosure. She breathed a sigh of relief.

B

Carefully, she placed the dish on the floor, her eyes never straying from the eyes of the wolf. Without a sound, she stepped, slowly, softly, before closing the gate to the enclosure. Only then did she breathe a sigh of relief.

a) Give three examples of how the cohesion has been improved in the second extract.

_____

_____

_____

3 marks

b) Find and copy the three-word alliteration from the text.

_____

1 mark

c) What do the words in the alliteration suggest about the character's feelings and actions?

_____

1 mark

II. **Read the extract.**

The sea glistened as gentle waves licked the shore. The golden sand led up to trees and shrubs with the steep, bumpy rocks beyond rising from the greenery like a herd of huge elephants. In the blue sky above, clouds drifted slowly and birds crowed and cawed as they circled the rocks.

a) Find and copy an example of a simile from the text.

_____

b) Find and copy an example of personification from the text.

_____

c) Find and copy an example of onomatopoeia from the text.

_____

3 marks

12. **Read the poem.**

Radiant sunset
A pink, stunning sky is still
As I watch and cry.

a) What type of poem is this?

_____

b) Find and copy an example of alliteration in the poem.

_____

2 marks

13. **Write the root word for each of the words below.**

a) unemployment _____

b) unfaithful _____

c) precautionary _____

d) uncoverable _____

4 marks

Total: [   ] /58 marks

Simplifying, comparing and ordering fractions

- Simplify fractions using common multiples to express fractions in the same denomination
- Compare and order fractions

Simplifying fractions

A **fraction** is a way of describing parts of a whole, whether it is a number, amount or shape. Different fractions can have the same value as each other; these are **equivalent fractions**.

Example

Each rectangle is the same, but divided into a different number of parts (fractions).

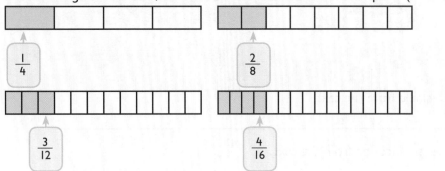

There is a pattern in the numerators and denominators.

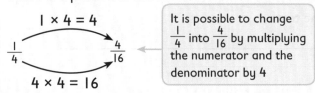

It is possible to change $\frac{1}{4}$ into $\frac{4}{16}$ by multiplying the numerator and the denominator by 4

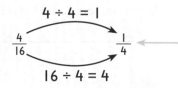

It is also possible to find equivalent fractions by dividing the numerator and denominator by a **common factor**.

When you make the value of the numerator and the denominator smaller (e.g. $\frac{4}{16} \Rightarrow \frac{1}{4}$), you are **simplifying** the fraction or reducing the fraction to its **simplest terms** (or lowest terms).

Comparing and ordering fractions

In order to compare fractions, the denominators must be the same.

Example

To compare $\frac{2}{3}$ and $\frac{5}{8}$, they must have the same denominator, so find the **lowest common multiple** of 3 and 8. This is 24

Find equivalent fractions for $\frac{2}{3}$ and $\frac{5}{8}$ that have denominators of 24.

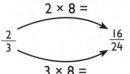

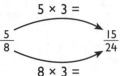

Once the fractions have the same denominator, they can be compared by their numerators.

$\frac{16}{24} > \frac{15}{24}$ so $\frac{2}{3} > \frac{5}{8}$

Once fractions have been compared, they can be put in order of size, largest or smallest first.

1. Complete these equivalent fractions.

$$\frac{2}{3} = \frac{\boxed{}}{6} = \frac{6}{\boxed{}} = \frac{\boxed{}}{12} = \frac{10}{\boxed{}} = \frac{\boxed{}}{18}$$

5 marks

2. Find the missing numerator or denominator.

a) $\frac{15}{20} = \frac{3}{\boxed{}}$ b) $\frac{15}{24} = \frac{\boxed{}}{8}$ c) $\frac{35}{50} = \frac{7}{\boxed{}}$

3 marks

3. Write these fractions in order, starting with the smallest.

$\frac{3}{4}$ $\frac{7}{12}$ $\frac{5}{6}$ $\frac{2}{3}$ $\boxed{}$ $\boxed{}$ $\boxed{}$ $\boxed{}$

1 mark

1. Find the missing numerator or denominator.

a) $\frac{32}{40} = \frac{4}{\boxed{}}$ b) $\frac{33}{45} = \frac{\boxed{}}{15}$

2 marks

2. Simplify: a) $\frac{21}{35} = \boxed{}$ b) $\frac{27}{63} = \boxed{}$

2 marks

3. Write these fractions in order, starting with the smallest.

$\frac{4}{5}$ $\frac{2}{3}$ $\frac{7}{10}$ $\frac{9}{15}$ $\boxed{}$ $\boxed{}$ $\boxed{}$ $\boxed{}$

1 mark

1. Simplify: a) $\frac{18}{81} = \boxed{}$ b) $\frac{48}{64} = \boxed{}$ c) $\frac{24}{72} = \boxed{}$ d) $\frac{18}{96} = \boxed{}$

4 marks

2. Write these fractions in order, starting with the smallest.

a) $\frac{2}{3}$ $\frac{5}{9}$ $\frac{7}{12}$ $\frac{3}{4}$ $\boxed{}$ $\boxed{}$ $\boxed{}$ $\boxed{}$

b) $\frac{5}{6}$ $\frac{3}{4}$ $\frac{3}{5}$ $\frac{2}{3}$ $\boxed{}$ $\boxed{}$ $\boxed{}$ $\boxed{}$

2 marks

PS 3. These fractions are in order, starting with the smallest. Find the missing fraction.

a) $\frac{4}{5}$ $\frac{\boxed{}}{20}$ $\frac{9}{10}$ b) $\frac{3}{8}$ $\frac{29}{\boxed{}}$ $\frac{4}{9}$ c) $\frac{1}{5}$ $\frac{13}{\boxed{}}$ $\frac{7}{30}$

3 marks

Total: $\boxed{}$ /23 marks

Had a go $\boxed{}$ **Getting there** $\boxed{}$ **Got it!** $\boxed{}$

Adding and subtracting fractions

- Add and subtract fractions

Adding fractions

When adding fractions, the **denominators** need to be the same. If the denominators are different, then an equivalent fraction must be used.

Example

$\frac{5}{6} + \frac{7}{12} =$

First, find the **lowest common multiple** of the fractions.

In this addition, the lowest common multiple of 6 and 12 is **12**:

Sixths can be changed into twelfths:
$\frac{5}{6} = \frac{10}{12}$

$\frac{10}{12} + \frac{7}{12} = \frac{17}{12} = 1\frac{5}{12}$

Sometimes, both denominators of the fractions to be added need to be changed. The lowest common multiple is still needed.

$\frac{4}{5} + \frac{1}{6} =$

In this addition, the lowest common multiple of 5 and 6 is **30**:

$\frac{24}{30} + \frac{5}{30} = \frac{29}{30}$

Sometimes, **mixed numbers** are used.

$2\frac{3}{4} + 3\frac{7}{10} =$

> Add the whole numbers. The lowest common multiple is 20.
> Then, add the fractions.

$5\frac{15}{20} + \frac{14}{20} = 5\frac{29}{20} = 5 + 1\frac{9}{20} = 6\frac{9}{20}$

> **Remember**
>
> Only ever add (or subtract) fractions that have the same denominators.

Subtracting fractions

Like addition, fractions can only be subtracted if they have the same denominator.

Both denominators of the fractions may need to be changed by finding the lowest common multiple.

Example

$\frac{4}{5} - \frac{2}{3} =$

The lowest common multiple of 5 and 3 is 15: $\frac{12}{15} - \frac{10}{15} = \frac{2}{15}$

Sometimes, mixed numbers are used.

$4\frac{3}{8} - 2\frac{2}{3} = 4\frac{9}{24} - 2\frac{16}{24}$ ← The lowest common multiple of 8 and 3 is 24

Change the mixed numbers into improper fractions. Then subtract the fractions:

$= \frac{105}{24} - \frac{64}{24} = \frac{41}{24} = 1\frac{17}{24}$

If the answer is an **improper fraction**, change it to a mixed number.
If the fraction can be **simplified**, reduce it to its lowest terms.

> **Key words**
>
> - denominator
> - lowest common multiple
> - mixed number
> - improper fraction
> - simplify

Challenge 1

1. a) $\frac{3}{4} + \frac{1}{8} = \boxed{}$ b) $\frac{2}{5} + \frac{3}{10} = \boxed{}$ c) $\frac{2}{3} + \frac{1}{4} = \boxed{}$ **3 marks**

2. a) $\frac{9}{10} - \frac{1}{2} = \boxed{}$ b) $\frac{2}{3} - \frac{1}{4} = \boxed{}$ c) $\frac{5}{6} - \frac{3}{4} = \boxed{}$ **3 marks**

PS 3. Jenny, Mia and Tom make cakes for a class party.

Jenny makes $\frac{1}{6}$ of the cakes and Mia makes $\frac{1}{3}$ of the cakes.

What fraction of the cakes does Tom make? $\boxed{}$

1 mark

Challenge 2

1. a) $\frac{1}{4} + \frac{1}{5} = \boxed{}$ b) $1\frac{5}{8} + 3\frac{2}{5} = \boxed{}$ c) $3\frac{2}{3} + 3\frac{1}{3} = \boxed{}$ **3 marks**

2. a) $\frac{9}{10} - \frac{1}{4} = \boxed{}$ b) $\frac{3}{5} - \frac{1}{3} = \boxed{}$ c) $2\frac{1}{12} - 1\frac{2}{3} = \boxed{}$ **3 marks**

PS 3. A pizza stall sells mushroom pizzas and four cheese pizzas by the slice.

At the end of the day, they have sold $8\frac{3}{8}$ of the mushroom pizzas and $6\frac{3}{4}$ of the four cheese pizzas.

How much more of the mushroom pizzas were sold? $\boxed{}$

1 mark

Challenge 3

1. a) $3\frac{2}{5} + 2\frac{5}{6} = \boxed{}$ b) $4\frac{3}{4} + 4\frac{7}{10} = \boxed{}$ c) $1\frac{2}{3} + 2\frac{3}{5} + 3\frac{5}{6} = \boxed{}$ **3 marks**

2. a) $4\frac{3}{10} - 2\frac{3}{4} = \boxed{}$ b) $2\frac{2}{3} - 1\frac{7}{8} = \boxed{}$ c) $1\frac{5}{8} - \frac{4}{5} = \boxed{}$ **3 marks**

PS 3. Find the missing denominator:

$2\frac{1}{2} + 2\frac{2}{3} + 1\frac{1}{\boxed{}} = 6\frac{5}{12}$

1 mark

PS 4. Find the missing numerator:

$3\frac{2}{3} - 1\frac{\boxed{}}{5} = 1\frac{13}{15}$

1 mark

PS 5. Find the missing mixed number:

$3\frac{2}{3} - 1\frac{5}{6} + \boxed{} = 3\frac{7}{12}$

1 mark

Total: $\boxed{}$ /23 marks

Had a go $\boxed{}$ **Getting there** $\boxed{}$ **Got it!** $\boxed{}$

Multiplying and dividing fractions

- Multiply and divide fractions by whole numbers

Multiplying fractions

To **multiply fractions**, you need to follow a number of stages.

Example

$\frac{1}{3} \times \frac{1}{4} =$

Think of this as $\frac{1}{4}$ of $\frac{1}{3}$

This rectangle is divided into thirds:

If this one-third was divided into four parts, it would show quarters of $\frac{1}{3}$

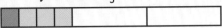

Dividing each third into quarters would mean there would be twelve parts.

$\frac{1}{3} \times \frac{1}{4} = \frac{1}{12}$

$\frac{2}{3} \times \frac{1}{4} =$

Think of this as $\frac{1}{4}$ of $\frac{2}{3}$

The rectangle shows $\frac{2}{3}$ divided into quarters. These thirds are divided into four parts, or quarters. The darker shading shows $\frac{1}{4}$ of $\frac{2}{3}$

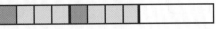

Two of the twelve parts show $\frac{1}{4}$ of $\frac{2}{3}$

$\frac{2}{3} \times \frac{1}{4} = \frac{2}{12} = \frac{1}{6}$

Dividing fractions

To **divide** fractions, you need to follow a number of stages.

Example

$\frac{1}{3} \div 4 =$

Think of this as $\frac{1}{3}$ divided into 4 parts:

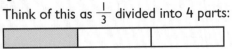

Dividing each third by 4 would mean there are twelve parts.

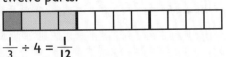

$\frac{1}{3} \div 4 = \frac{1}{12}$

$\frac{2}{3} \div 4 =$

Think of this as $\frac{2}{3}$ and each divided into 4 parts.

Dividing each third by 4 would mean there are twelve parts.

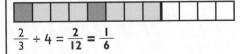

$\frac{2}{3} \div 4 = \frac{2}{12} = \frac{1}{6}$

> **Tip**
>
> Dividing by a fraction is the same as multiplying by an inverted fraction.

Quick ways to multiply and divide fractions

The quickest way to multiply fractions is:

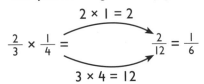

$$2 \times 1 = 2$$
$$\frac{2}{3} \times \frac{1}{4} = \frac{2}{12} = \frac{1}{6}$$
$$3 \times 4 = 12$$

The quickest way to divide a fraction is:

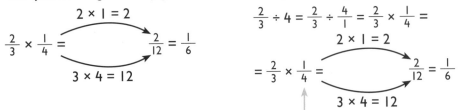

$$\frac{2}{3} \div 4 = \frac{2}{3} \div \frac{4}{1} = \frac{2}{3} \times \frac{1}{4} =$$

$$2 \times 1 = 2$$
$$= \frac{2}{3} \times \frac{1}{4} = \frac{2}{12} = \frac{1}{6}$$
$$3 \times 4 = 12$$

> $4 = \frac{4}{1}$ and the quick way to divide by a fraction is to flip it and multiply. Then multiply the numerators and multiply the denominators.

> **Key words**
>
> - multiplication
> - fraction
> - division

Challenge 1

1. a) $\frac{1}{2} \times \frac{1}{5} =$ ☐　　b) $\frac{1}{5} \times \frac{1}{3} =$ ☐　　c) $\frac{1}{6} \times \frac{1}{4} =$ ☐　　 3 marks

2. a) $\frac{1}{3} \div 4 =$ ☐　　b) $\frac{1}{5} \div 2 =$ ☐　　c) $\frac{1}{6} \div 5 =$ ☐　　 3 marks

PS 3. Max buys a pack of football cards. $\frac{1}{2}$ of the cards show footballers. Of those cards, $\frac{3}{4}$ are in colour.

What fraction of the pack shows footballers on coloured cards? ☐　 1 mark

Challenge 2

1. a) $\frac{2}{3} \times \frac{1}{6} =$ ☐　　b) $\frac{3}{5} \times \frac{3}{4} =$ ☐　　c) $\frac{3}{10} \times \frac{4}{5} =$ ☐　　 3 marks

2. a) $\frac{3}{8} \div 4 =$ ☐　　b) $\frac{5}{6} \div 5 =$ ☐　　c) $\frac{3}{4} \div 6 =$ ☐　　 3 marks

PS 3. Kate has some homework for the weekend. She does some homework on Friday night but leaves $\frac{7}{8}$ of her homework for Saturday and Sunday. She divides the homework equally between the two days.

What fraction of her homework does she do on Sunday? ☐　 1 mark

Challenge 3

1. Find the missing fraction:

   a) $\frac{1}{8} \times$ ☐ $= \frac{1}{24}$　　b) $\frac{2}{5} \times$ ☐ $= \frac{2}{15}$　　c) $\frac{3}{5} \times$ ☐ $= \frac{2}{5}$　　3 marks

2. Find the missing number:

   a) $\frac{1}{8} \div$ ☐ $= \frac{1}{40}$　　b) $\frac{2}{5} \div$ ☐ $= \frac{2}{15}$　　c) $\frac{4}{5} \div$ ☐ $= \frac{1}{5}$　　3 marks

PS 3. Maya buys 5 pizzas for a party. At the end of the party, there are $\frac{3}{8}$ of each pizza left.

What is the equivalent amount of pizzas left over? ☐　 1 mark

PS 4. Sukhi has used $\frac{1}{5}$ of a bag of flour. She uses the rest equally to make 3 cakes.

What fraction of the bag of flour is used for each cake? ☐　 1 mark

Total: ☐ /22 marks

Had a go ☐　　**Getting there** ☐　　**Got it!** ☐

Decimal, fraction and percentage equivalents

- Know the place value of decimals and multiply and divide decimals by 10, 100 and 1,000
- Use a fraction to calculate a decimal equivalent
- Know percentage equivalents for fractions and decimals

Place value of decimals

Just like whole numbers, **decimals** have a place value too.

Thousands	Hundreds	Tens	Ones	•	tenths	hundredths	thousandths
4	7	8	0	•	2	6	3

> The **decimal point** is used to separate whole numbers from the parts of whole numbers (the decimals).
> Here, the digit 2 has a place value of 2 tenths or $\frac{2}{10}$ and as a decimal it is written as 0.2

Moving a digit one column to the right makes its value ten times smaller, and moving the digit two columns to the right makes its value one hundred times smaller, e.g.

$5 \div 10 = 0.5$

$5 \div 100 = 0.05$

$5 \div 1,000 = 0.005$

Moving a digit one column to the left makes its value ten times greater, and moving the digit two columns to the left makes its value one hundred times greater, e.g.

$1.002 \times 10 = 10.02$

$1.002 \times 100 = 100.2$

$1.002 \times 1,000 = 1,002$

Fraction and decimal equivalents

The **fraction** equivalent of a decimal can be found by using the place value, e.g.

$0.9 = \frac{9}{10}$ $0.07 = \frac{7}{100}$ $0.003 = \frac{3}{1,000}$ $0.37 = \frac{37}{100}$ $0.109 = \frac{109}{1,000}$

Sometimes, it will be possible to simplify the fraction, e.g. $0.45 = \frac{45}{100} = \frac{9}{20}$

A decimal equivalent of a fraction can be found by dividing the **numerator** by the **denominator**.

> **Tip**
>
> Learning simple fraction, decimal and percentage equivalents saves having to calculate each time.

Example

$\frac{4}{5} = 0.8$ $\frac{3}{8} = 0.375$ $\frac{1}{3} = 0.\overline{3}$

$$\begin{array}{r} 0 \cdot 8 \\ 5 \overline{) 4 \cdot {}^4 0} \end{array}$$

$$\begin{array}{r} 0 \cdot 3\ 7\ 5 \\ 8 \overline{) 3 \cdot {}^3 0\ {}^6 0\ {}^4 0} \end{array}$$

$$\begin{array}{r} 0 \cdot 3\ 3\ 3 \\ 3 \overline{) 1 \cdot {}^1 0\ {}^1 0\ {}^1 0} \end{array}$$

> This fraction does not have an exact decimal equivalent.
> This is 0.3 **recurring** or $0.\overline{3}$

Fraction, decimal and percentage equivalents

Example

5% is '5 out of 100'.

This can be written as a fraction: $\frac{5}{100}$ simplifying to $\frac{1}{20}$ and as a decimal $\frac{5}{100} = 0.05$

Further examples are: $60\% = \frac{60}{100} \left(= \frac{3}{5}\right) = 0.6$ $85\% = \frac{85}{100} \left(= \frac{17}{20}\right) = 0.85$

> **Key words**
>
> - decimal
> - decimal point
> - fraction
> - numerator
> - denominator
> - recurring

Challenge 1

1. a) **52.83**   What is the value of the digit 3? _____

    b) **163.79**   What is the value of the digit 7? _____

    c) **5.062**   What is the value of the digit 2? _____

    3 marks

2. a) $5.1 \div 10 =$ _____   b) $5.98 \times 100 =$ _____

    c) $261.9 \div 100 =$ _____   d) $9.063 \times 10 =$ _____

    4 marks

3. Complete the missing fraction and decimal equivalents to the percentages.

    a) $90\% =$ ☐ $=$ ☐   b) $35\% =$ ☐ $=$ ☐

    c) $75\% =$ ☐ $=$ ☐   d) $40\% =$ ☐ $=$ ☐

    8 marks

Challenge 2

1. a) $2.07 \div 10 =$ _____   b) $0.604 \times 1,000 =$ _____

    c) $431 \div 1,000 =$ _____   d) $0.078 \times 100 =$ _____

    4 marks

2. Complete the missing fractions and decimal equivalents to the percentages.

    a) $15\% =$ ☐ $=$ ☐   b) $12\% =$ ☐ $=$ ☐

    c) $72\% =$ ☐ $=$ ☐   d) $65\% =$ ☐ $=$ ☐

    8 marks

PS 3. The gauge on an oil tank is showing that it is $\frac{3}{20}$ full.

    What is this as a percentage? ☐

    1 mark

Challenge 3

1. Find the missing number:

    a) $40.25 \div$ ☐ $= 4.025$ b) $0.083 \times$ ☐ $= 83$

    2 marks

2. Complete the missing decimal and percentage equivalents to the fractions.

    a) $\frac{2}{5} =$ ☐ $=$ ☐   b) $\frac{24}{25} =$ ☐ $=$ ☐

    c) $\frac{3}{50} =$ ☐ $=$ ☐   d) $\frac{11}{20} =$ ☐ $=$ ☐

    8 marks

PS 3. Samir is promoted at work. His pay increases by $\frac{1}{8}$

    What is this as a percentage? ☐

    1 mark

Total: ☐ /39 marks

Had a go ☐   **Getting there** ☐   **Got it!** ☐

71

Calculating with decimals

- Multiply 1-digit numbers with up to two decimal places by whole numbers
- Divide numbers that give answers with up to two decimal places

Multiplying decimals

A 1-digit number with up to two **decimal places** is a number such as 0.6 or 0.07

Example

0.6 × 7 =	0.6 is ten times less than 6	(6 ÷ 10 = 0.6)
	So, 0.6 × 7 =	
	6 × 7 ÷ 10 =	
	42 ÷ 10 =	
	4.2	
0.07 × 4 =	0.07 is a hundred times less than 7	(7 ÷ 100 = 0.07)
	So, 0.07 × 4 =	
	7 × 4 ÷ 100 =	
	28 ÷ 100 =	
	0.28	

> **Tip**
>
> Many of these calculations can be completed mentally but depend on a good recall of multiplication facts.

To complete the multiplication of 1-digit numbers with one decimal place mentally, use the key multiplication fact and divide the answer by ten: 0.9 × 3 = 2.7

To complete the multiplication of 1-digit numbers with two decimal places mentally, use the key multiplication fact and divide the answer by a hundred: 0.09 × 3 = 0.27

If the whole number is a 2-digit number, **partition** the whole number.

Example

0.08 × 43 =   8 × 40 ÷ 100 = 320 ÷ 100 = 3.2
8 × 3 ÷ 100 = 24 ÷ 100 = 0.24   ⟵   Multiply by 40 and multiply by 3 separately.
3.2 + 0.24 = 3.44

Dividing decimals

Not all divisions give a whole number answer; many do not. If there is a remainder, this can be used to calculate a more exact answer by using extra zeros in the tenth, hundredth and, if needed, thousandth columns, and continuing the division.

Example

32 ÷ 5 =	634 ÷ 8 =
$\begin{array}{r} 6 \cdot 4 \\ \hline 5\,|\,3\ 2 \cdot \overset{2}{0} \end{array}$	$\begin{array}{r} 7\ 9 \cdot 2\ 5 \\ \hline 8\,|\,6\ 3\ \overset{7}{4} \cdot \overset{2}{0}\ \overset{4}{0} \end{array}$
32 ÷ 5 = **6.4**	634 ÷ 8 = **79.25**
28 ÷ 9 =	**57 ÷ 11 =**
$\begin{array}{r} 3 \cdot 1\ 1\ 1 \\ \hline 9\,|\,2\ 8 \cdot \overset{1}{0}\ \overset{1}{0}\ \overset{1}{0} \end{array}$	$\begin{array}{r} 5 \cdot 1\ 8\ 1\ 8 \\ \hline 11\,|\,5\ 7 \cdot \overset{2}{0}\ \overset{9}{0}\ \overset{2}{0}\ \overset{9}{0} \end{array}$
28 ÷ 9 = **3.$\overline{1}$**	57 ÷ 11 = **5.$\overline{18}$**

> **Key words**
>
> - decimal place
> - partition
> - recurring

> The '1' and '8' are **recurring** so they are written with a bar above them.

Challenge 1

1. a) $0.6 \times 7 =$ _____

    b) $0.9 \times 4 =$ _____

    c) $0.3 \times 8 =$ _____

    d) $0.07 \times 4 =$ _____

2. a) $37 \div 2 =$ _____

    b) $41 \div 5 =$ _____

    c) $34 \div 4 =$ _____

    d) $63 \div 4 =$ _____

PS 3. Paul buys 7 bags of flour that each hold 0.5 kg of flour.

   What is the mass of flour that Paul buys?

   ☐ kg

Challenge 2

1. a) $0.09 \times 8 =$ _____

    b) $0.07 \times 8 =$ _____

    c) $0.3 \times 15 =$ _____

    d) $0.05 \times 33 =$ _____

2. a) $347 \div 2 =$ _____

    b) $164 \div 5 =$ _____

    c) $223 \div 4 =$ _____

    d) $130 \div 8 =$ _____

PS 3. Simon and three friends wash cars and earn £87.

   They share the money equally.

   How much do they each get?

   £ _____

Challenge 3

1. Find the missing number:

    a) $0.7 \times$ ☐ $= 8.4$

    b) $0.06 \times$ ☐ $= 0.54$

    c) ☐ $\times 4 = 0.48$

    d) ☐ $\times 15 = 0.3$

    e) ☐ $\div 4 = 3.75$

    f) ☐ $\div 5 = 6.8$

PS 2. A group of 17 friends share taxis to go into town. A taxi can hold 5 people.

   How many taxis do they need?

   ☐

3. Calculate these divisions that give answers with recurring decimals.

    a) $49 \div 3 =$ _____

    b) $85 \div 6 =$ _____

Total: ☐ **/27 marks**

Had a go ☐   **Getting there** ☐   **Got it!** ☐

Scaling and scale factors

- Solve problems involving relative sizes
- Use scale factors

Scaling

Some problems involve finding missing numbers by looking at two related quantities using multiplication or division.

Example

This calculation uses **multiplication**:

If 5 apples cost £1.28, how much do 30 apples cost?

Every five apples cost £1.28, so calculate how many fives there are in 30
(30 ÷ 5 = 6)

Each of the 6 groups (of 5 apples) will cost £1.28, so calculate
£1.28 × 6   (1.28 × 6 = 7.68)

Answer: 30 apples cost **£7.68**

This calculation uses **division**:

A custard recipe uses 14 eggs for 35 people. How many eggs will be needed for 5 people?

14 eggs are needed for 35 people so calculate how many fives are in 35   (35 ÷ 5 = 7)

The number of eggs must be reduced by 7 times
(14 ÷ 7 = 2)

Answer: **2** eggs will be needed for 5 people

> ### Remember
> Remember, scaling and scale factors are always based on multiplication and division.

Scale factors

Scale factors are used in the same way but are often applied to shapes.

Example

These three triangles are **similar**; this means they are the same shape but have different measurements.

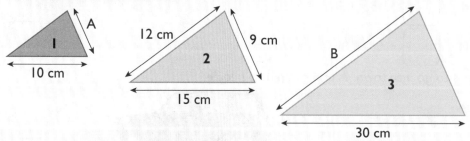

Find the lengths of sides A and B.

In Triangle 2, all the measurements are shown. In Triangle 1 only the base length, 10 cm is given. This is $\frac{2}{3}$ of the base length on Triangle 2. So, Side A will be $\frac{2}{3}$ of the equivalent side of Triangle 2:

$\frac{2}{3}$ of 9 = 6   **Answer:** Side A is **6 cm**

In Triangle 3, the base length is also the only given length. It is twice the length of Triangle 2. So, Side B will be twice the length of the equivalent length of Triangle 2:

12 × 2 = 24   **Answer:** Side B is **24 cm**

> ### Key words
> - scale factor
> - similar

Challenge 1

PS 1. If 6 bananas cost £2.50, how much would you pay for:

    a) 3 bananas? £ _____

    b) 12 bananas? £ _____

2 marks

2. Here are three similar rectangles.

    a) What is the length of Side A? ☐ cm

    b) What is the length of Side B? ☐ cm

2 marks

Challenge 2

PS 1. Dan works for 3 hours and earns £70; how much will he earn if he works for:

    a) 6 hours? £ _____   **b)** 24 hours? £ _____   **c)** 36 hours? £ _____

3 marks

2. Here are three similar triangles.

    a) What is the length of Side A? ☐ cm

    b) What is the length of Side B? ☐ cm

2 marks

Challenge 3

1. If a car factory can build 130 cars in four hours, how many complete cars can be built in:

    a) 6 hours? _____   **b)** 10 hours? _____

2 marks

2. A rectangle is 40 cm long and 25 cm wide. A similar rectangle has a length of 60 cm.

    How wide is the larger rectangle?

    _____ cm

1 mark

3. A parallelogram has sides of 21 cm and 15 cm. A similar, smaller parallelogram has a shorter side of 10 cm.

    What is the length of the longer side of the smaller parallelogram?

    _____ cm

1 mark

Total: ☐ / 13 marks

Had a go ☐   **Getting there** ☐   **Got it!** ☐

Percentages and unequal sharing

- Calculate using percentages
- Share unequally

Using percentages

Per cent means 'out of one hundred'. So, 20% (20 per cent) means 20 out of 100. This can be written as $\frac{20}{100}$, which **simplifies** to $\frac{2}{10}$ and then to $\frac{1}{5}$. As a **decimal** this is 0.2

There are different ways to find a percentage of a number, amount or a shape.

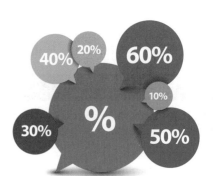

Example

Find 20% of 45

Find $\frac{1}{5}$ of 45   → This is 45 ÷ 5 = **9**

Find 0.2 of 45   → This is 45 × 0.2 = **9**

Or using the '10% method' (10% = $\frac{1}{10}$)

20% = 10% + 10%, so find 2 × ($\frac{1}{10}$ of 45) → 2 (45 ÷ 10) = 2 × 4.5 = **9**

Generally, using the '10% method' allows for mental methods, probably supported by jotting or note-taking:

Find 35% of 48

35% = 10% + 10% + 10% + 5%

10% of 48 = 4.8

5% of 48 = 2.4   ← | 5% is half of 10%, so, 5% of 48 is half of 10% of 48 |

35% of 48 = 4.8 + 4.8 + 4.8 + 2.4 = **16.8**

Unequal sharing

Dividing by a number divides the number into equal groups, but numbers and quantities are not always shared **equally**. They can be shared **unequally**.

Example

Ben and Mo share £45 so that Mo gets twice as much as Ben.

As a picture, this could be shown as:

Ben's share = ●

Mo's share = ● ●

Altogether, there are 3 shares. The calculation is 45 ÷ 3 = 15

Ben gets one share: **£15**

Mo gets two shares: £15 × 2 = **£30**

This can also be calculated as a **ratio**.

Ben and Mo share £45 in the ratio of 1 : 2 ← | This is the ratio, said as 'one to two'. |

It is calculated in the same way.

The ratio is 1 : 2, which is three shares as 1 + 2 = 3

45 ÷ 3 = 15 ← | Each share is worth £15 |

Ben has 1 share: **£15**; Mo has 2 shares: **£30**

Keeping numbers in **proportion** is similar and means the ratio of 1 : 2 is the same as 2 : 4 or 3 : 6

> **Tip**
>
> If you are unsure, think of unequal sharing or ratios as a picture.

> **Key words**
>
> - per cent
> - simplify
> - decimal
> - ratio
> - proportion

Challenge 1

1. a) 10% of 200 = ☐   b) 25% of 80 = ☐   c) 50% of 150 = ☐

   3 marks

PS 2. Poppy completes a maths test of fifty 1-mark questions. She gets a mark of 80%

   How many questions did Poppy get right? ☐   *1 mark*

3. Divide:

   a) 30 in the ratio of 2 : 1 ☐ and ☐   b) 50 in the ratio of 4 : 1 ☐ and ☐

   2 marks

PS 4. Jenny mixes juice and water in the ratio of 1 : 7 to make 400 ml of drink.

   How much water does Jenny add to the juice? _____ ml   *1 mark*

Challenge 2

1. a) 15% of 120 = ☐   b) 95% of 80 = ☐   c) 70% of 240 = ☐

   3 marks

PS 2. Teddy earns £320 a week. He gets a 5% pay rise.

   How much extra will he earn each week? £ ☐   *1 mark*

3. Divide these numbers in the ratio:

   a) 140 in the ratio of 4 : 3 ☐ and ☐

   b) 350 in the ratio of 2 : 3 ☐ and ☐

   2 marks

PS 4. Dave and Amy share £90 so that Amy has three times as much as Dave.

   How much does Amy get?   £ _____   *1 mark*

Challenge 3

PS 1. Chen finds 40% of a number. Chen's answer is 90

   What was the number? _____   *1 mark*

PS 2. Jay and Javid complete a test of 20 1-mark questions.

   Jay scores 60% in the test. Javid gets $\frac{13}{20}$ in the same test.

   How many more marks did Javid get than Jay? ☐   *1 mark*

PS 3. Jacob uses flour, butter and sugar for cakes in the ratio of 4 : 6 : 7

   He uses 200 g of flour. How much butter and sugar will he use?

   Butter: _____ g

   Sugar: _____ g   *2 marks*

PS 4. Laura mixes juice and water in the ratio of 1 : 5 using 480 ml more water than juice.

   How much drink did Laura make?

   _____ ml   *1 mark*

Total: ☐ / 19 marks

Had a go ☐   **Getting there** ☐   **Got it!** ☐

Equations and formulae

- Express missing number problems algebraically
- Use simple formulae
- Generate and describe linear sequences

Missing number problems

In algebra, missing number problems use **unknowns**. The unknown is a specific number. Equations use symbols or letters to represent the unknown.

Example

Nishi has a secret number. She adds 12 to her number. The answer is 20

This can be written algebraically as: $s + 12 = 20$ ← | s stands for the secret number.

Find the value of s by subtracting 12 from 20: $20 - 12 = 8$ $s = 8$

> **Remember**
>
> In algebra, multiplications and divisions are usually written without multiplication or division signs, e.g.
>
> $3a = 3 \times a$
> $\frac{b}{5} = b \div 5$, $\frac{10}{c} = 10 \div c$

Using formulae

Formulae are an abbreviated set of instructions to solve a problem. They use **variables** to stand for any number. The variables may change.

Example

A plumber works out her fees by multiplying the number of hours by £25 and adding a call-out charge of £30 and the cost of any parts she uses.

This can be abbreviated into the formula: $f = 25h + 30 + p$ ← | f = fees h = hours p = parts

h and p are variables; they will both change according to the job the plumber is working on.

25 and 30 are **constants** because they will always stay the same; she always charges £25 an hour and £30 for a call-out.

The plumber will work out the cost by **substitution**. When she knows the number of hours and the cost of the parts, she will substitute these values for h and p. So, if the number of hours worked is 5 and the cost of parts is £40, the calculation is:

$25 \times 5 + 30 + 40 = 195$ ← | The plumber will charge £195

Linear sequences

Linear sequences are based on multiplication.

6   12   18   24 ← | This is a '+ 6' sequence, but also shows the multiples of 6

The formula describing the sequence is: $n = 6x$ ←

The 4th number in the sequence = $6 \times 4 = 24$ | x is the number in the sequence.

7   13   19   25 ← | This is also a '+ 6' sequence but adds 1 more.

The formula describing the sequence is:

   $n = 6x + 1$

   The 4th number is $6 \times 4 + 1 = 25$

   The 5th number is $6 \times 5 + 1 = 31$

This is sometimes called 'finding the nth **term**'.

> **Key words**
>
> - unknown
> - formula
> - variable
> - constant
> - substitution
> - linear sequence
> - n^th term

Challenge 1

1. Circle the expression that shows that 5 times greater than a number is 45

   5n   5n = 45   n + 5 = 45   45 − n = 5   5 × 45 = 225

   1 mark

PS 2. A taxi driver works out the cost of his fares in £ using this formula:

   $f = 1m + 3$ (f = the fare, m = the journey in miles, 3 = a standing charge)

   Work out the cost of a fare if the journey is 5 miles.

   1 mark

3. Here is a linear number sequence: 4   7   10   13   16

   Circle the description of the sequence.

   $n = 4x$ $n = 3x$ $n = 3x + 4$ $n = 3x + 1$ $n = 2x − 2$

   1 mark

Challenge 2

1. Write these problems algebraically using a letter n for the missing value.

   a) 50 divided by a number is 25 _____

   b) 15 multiplied by a number is 90 _____

   2 marks

PS 2. A bus company uses this formula to work out the cost (in £) of hiring a bus:

   $C = 2m + 30h + 75$ (C = cost of the hire, m = length of the journey in miles, h = number of hours of hire, 75 is a standing charge)

   Work out the cost of hiring a bus for a journey of 5 hours and 80 miles.

   _____

   1 mark

3. The formula for a number sequence is $n = 5x − 2$

   a) What is the 6th number in the sequence?

   b) What is the 12th number in the sequence?

   2 marks

Challenge 3

1. Using a letter n for the missing value, write '4 less than a number is 95' algebraically. _____

   1 mark

PS 2. A teacher works out the total marks for three tasks using this formula: $m = \frac{a}{2} + b + 2c$

   (m = total marks, a = score for 1st task, b = score for 2nd task, c = score for 3rd task)

   Work out Dev's total marks if he got 24 for the 1st task, 25 for the 2nd task and 18 for the 3rd task.

   [ ] marks

   1 mark

3. a) What is the formula for this sequence?   7   15   23   31 _____

   b) What is the formula for this sequence?   8   13   18   23 _____

   2 marks

Total: [   ] / 12 marks

Had a go [ ]   Getting there [ ]   Got it! [ ]

79

Unknowns and variables

- Solve equations with two unknowns
- Find possibilities for combinations of two variables

Equations with two unknowns

An equation may have two **unknowns**. There will be a specific value for each unknown.

Example

$m + n = 12$ and $m - n = 8$

$m + n = 12$ has a number of possible solutions ($1 + 11$, $-1 + 13$, $6 + 6$, $\frac{1}{4} + 11\frac{3}{4}$), but only one of these possible solutions will lead to $m - n = 8$

The values for m and n must be the same in both equations.

Answer: m must be 10 and n must be 2 ← | $10 + 2 = 12$ and $10 - 2 = 8$ |

Bryn takes two parcels to the Post Office. Together, the parcels have a mass of 15 kg but one parcel is 3 kg greater than the other. What is the mass of the heavier parcel?

This can be calculated as $15 - 3 = 12$ ← | This removes the difference. |

Next $12 \div 2$ divides the mass between the two parcels.

Add 3 to one of the values: $6 + 3 = 9$ ← | This adds the difference back again. |

Answer: The heavier parcel is 9 kg.

Combinations of variables

An equation may have two **variables**. These are values that could be different and there is more than one possible answer.

Example

$m + n = 12$

Without the second equation of $m - n = 8$, there will be an infinite number of possible answers.

Solutions could be:

$1 + 11 = 12$ $-1 + 13 = 12$ $0.5 + 11.5 = 12$ $1\frac{1}{2} + 10\frac{1}{2} = 12$

Rules could be imposed, e.g. $m + n = 12$ and m and n are positive odd numbers, which would limit the number of answers to six possible combinations:

$1 + 11 = 12$ $3 + 9 = 12$ $5 + 7 = 12$ $7 + 5 = 12$ $9 + 3 = 12$ $11 + 1 = 12$

Some friends go to a café and buy teas and coffees. They spend £8 and buy 5 drinks. How many teas and how many coffees could they have bought?

Find five numbers that total 8. There are many possible answers, e.g. If 1 tea costs **£2**, each coffee would cost **£1.50**   ($8 - 2 = 6$ and $6 \div 4 = 1.5$)

If 2 teas cost **£1.45** each, each coffee would cost **£1.70** ($1.45 \times 2 = 2.90$ $8 - 2.90 = 5.10$ $5.10 \div 3 = 1.70$)

Tip

It is a good idea to use the facts that have been given and ask, "What could the answer be?". Work out the possibilities, then check that the solution matches the demands of the question.

Key words

- unknown
- variable

Challenge 1

1. These shapes represent numbers.

   ■ + ● = 30   ■ – ● = 28

   Find the value of the shapes.

   ■ = ☐   ● = ☐

   1 mark

PS 2. Larry fills two bottles with 2 litres of water. One bottle holds 400 ml more than the other.

How much water is in the larger bottle? _____ ml

1 mark

3. a and b are positive whole numbers. Give three possible values of a and b if $a - b = 6$

_____   _____   _____

3 marks

PS 4. Jo has £30 in £5 and £10 notes. Give the two combinations of the £5 and £10 notes Jo has.

_____

_____

2 marks

Challenge 2

1. If $c \times d = 24$ and $c + d = 14$, find the value of c and d. $c =$ ☐ $d =$ ☐

1 mark

PS 2. Josh buys a 2 metre length of wood. He cuts it into three pieces. Each of the two pieces are half the length of the third piece.

How long is the longest piece of wood? _____ m

1 mark

3. The values in this equation are positive whole numbers: $e + e + e + f + f = 48$

Find a possible pair of values for e and f. $e =$ ☐ $f =$ ☐

1 mark

PS 4. Mia buys three identical pencils and a pen. A pen costs more than a pencil. The pen costs more than 30p and the pencils cost more than 10p each. She spends 80p.

Find two possible values in pence for the pencil and pen.

pen = ☐ pencil = ☐   pen = ☐ pencil = ☐

2 marks

Challenge 3

1. Use these two equations to find the value of g and h: $g - 7 = 18$ $g \times h = 125$

$g =$ ☐ $h =$ ☐

1 mark

PS 2. Fay has £5, £10 and £20 notes. She has 3 of one kind, 2 of another and 1 of the third. If she has £65, how many of each note does she have?

_____

1 mark

3. j and k are positive and different whole numbers: $3j + \dfrac{k}{2} = 20$

Find a set of values for j and k. $j =$ ☐ $k =$ ☐

1 mark

PS 4. 25 children are divided into 3 larger and equal groups and 2 smaller and equal groups. How many children are in each group?

_____

1 mark

Total: ☐ / 16 marks

Had a go ☐   **Getting there** ☐   **Got it!** ☐

Progress test 4

1. Try to calculate these mentally.

   a) 38 + 39 = [ ]

   b) 45 × 7 = [ ]

   c) 2,000 − 220 = [ ]

   d) 78 ÷ 6 = [ ]

   4 marks

PS 2. A theme park was visited by 862 people on Friday, 1,382 on Saturday and 1,734 on Sunday.

   How many people visited altogether over the three days? [ ]

   1 mark

3. a) 6,230 ÷ 7 = [ ]

   b) 68 × 68 = [ ]

   c) 4,715 ÷ 23 = [ ]

   3 marks

4. Circle the fraction that is different when reduced to its lowest terms.

   $\frac{45}{60}$　　$\frac{27}{36}$　　$\frac{36}{48}$　　$\frac{52}{65}$　　$\frac{60}{80}$

   1 mark

PS 5. Manisha buys 7 oranges for £2.75

   a) How much would she pay for 21 oranges?　£ [ ]

   b) How much would she pay for 35 oranges?　£ [ ]

   2 marks

6. Write these problems algebraically, using *n* for the unknown values.

   a) 12 less than a number is 34 _____

   b) a number divided by 8 equals 64 _____

   c) 56 more than a number is 78 _____

   d) a number multiplied by 16 equals 896 _____

   4 marks

7. Complete this table by rounding the numbers.

		Round to the nearest 1,000	Round to the nearest 100,000	Round to the nearest 1,000,000
a)	4,092,781			
b)	6,937,095			
c)	8,249,811			

   9 marks

PS 8. A gardener buys 35 bags of bulbs. Each bag holds 150 bulbs.

   He plants 800 bulbs in each of 6 flower beds.

   How many bulbs does he have left? [ ]

   1 mark

82

9. Write two million, six hundred and five thousand and seventy in figures.

_____

1 mark

PS 10. The temperature in the freezer compartment of a fridge is −18 °C.

The temperature in the kitchen is 23 °C.

What is the difference between the two temperatures? ☐ °C

1 mark

11. Write these numbers in order, starting with the largest.

624,923   624,135   625,138   626,091   626,022

_____   _____   _____   _____   _____

largest   **smallest**

1 mark

12. a) Circle the numbers that are **not** common multiples of 8 and 12

    24   36   48   72   108

b) Circle the numbers that are **not** common factors of 96 and 120

    4   8   16   24   32

c) Circle the numbers that are **not** prime numbers.

    47   57   67   77   87

3 marks

PS 13. Jay has $\frac{3}{4}$ of a pizza left over. He divides the pizza between himself and a friend.

What fraction of the whole pizza do they each get? ☐

1 mark

14. Complete this table showing fraction, decimal and percentage equivalents.

Fraction		Decimal		Percentage
$\frac{2}{5}$	=		=	
	=	0.05	=	
	=		=	4%
$\frac{23}{50}$	=		=	

8 marks

PS 15. Five friends buy a present for another friend.
They share the cost equally.

The present costs £32
How much does each friend pay? £ ☐

1 mark

16. a) 60 + 90 ÷ 10 + 20 = ☐

b) (60 + 90) ÷ 10 + 20 = ☐

2 marks

17. a) Circle the number where the digit 4 has a place value of forty thousand.

    401,540   1,400,800   40,840   4,084,404   1,480,329

b) Circle the number where the digit 5 has a place value of five hundred thousand.

    5,003,470   750,004   2,506,780   45,004   3,157,982

2 marks

18. a) $\dfrac{3}{4} + \dfrac{1}{6} =$ ☐ b) $\dfrac{7}{8} - \dfrac{1}{3} =$ ☐ c) $3\dfrac{2}{3} - 2\dfrac{3}{4} =$ ☐

3 marks

PS 19. **Dev is completing some calculations. He estimates the answers first by rounding.**

a) **4,634 + 3,578 =** Dev rounds each number to the nearest thousand.

What is Dev's estimated answer? _____

b) **719 × 56 =** Dev rounds 719 to the nearest hundred and 56 to the nearest ten.

What is Dev's estimated answer? _____

c) **7,425 ÷ 45 =** Dev rounds 7,425 to the nearest thousand and 45 to the nearest ten.

What is Dev's estimated answer? _____

3 marks

20. **Write these fractions in order, starting with the smallest.**

$\dfrac{27}{40}$ $\dfrac{5}{8}$ $\dfrac{7}{10}$ $\dfrac{13}{20}$ $\dfrac{3}{5}$

☐ ☐ ☐ ☐ ☐

smallest **largest**

1 mark

PS 21. **Max makes a scale model aeroplane. The scale is 2 cm to 1.5 m. The model has a length of 18 cm.**

What is the length of the actual aeroplane?

☐ m

1 mark

PS 22. **Lily and Gill work for the same company. They both earn £18,000 a year.**

Lily is promoted at work and gets a 20% pay rise. Gill just gets an annual pay rise of 5%

How much more does Lily earn in a year than Gill?

£ ☐

1 mark

23. **These three triangles are all similar.**

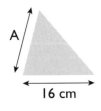

A

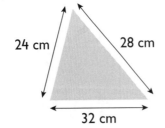

24 cm 28 cm

32 cm

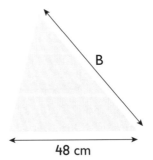

B

48 cm

16 cm

a) What is the length of Side A? ☐ cm

b) What is the length of Side B? ☐ cm

2 marks

PS 24. Kyle, Javid and Joe have been gardening for some neighbours. They have earned £120 altogether.

They all worked for different lengths of time. Kyle worked three times longer than Joe, and Javid worked twice as long as Joe. They divide the money according to the hours they have worked.

How much do they each earn?

Kyle = [   ]   Javid = [   ]   Joe = [   ]

[   ] 3 marks

PS 25. Janet makes bracelets. She uses a formula to work out the price, in pence, she should sell the bracelets for:

P = 10 + 40s + 50g   (P stands for the final price, s stands for silver beads, g stands for gold beads and 10 covers the cost of the thread.)

Find the cost of the following bracelets. Give your answer in £.

a)   A bracelet with 20 silver beads and no gold beads. [   ]

b)   A bracelet with 15 silver beads and 5 gold beads. [   ]

[   ] 2 marks

26. Find possible values for a and b in this equation:

4a + b = 21

a = [   ] b = [   ]

[   ] 2 marks

PS 27. Pippa buys three coffees and two teas for £18

The coffees are twice the price of a tea.

What is the cost of one coffee?

£ [   ]

[   ] 1 mark

PS 28. Tables of eight are set out in the school hall for lunch.

There are 235 children having lunch.

What is the minimum number of tables needed for the children?

[   ]

[   ] 1 mark

29. Find the missing numbers.

a) $0.5 \times$ [   ] $= 4$ b) $0.07 \times$ [   ] $= 5.6$ c) [   ] $\times 9 = 0.45$

[   ] 3 marks

PS 30. Ned fills 20 glasses with juice. Each glass is filled with $\frac{1}{8}$ litre of juice.

How much juice, in litres, does Ned use?

[   ] l

[   ] 1 mark

31. Find the missing numerator or denominator in these calculations.

a) $\frac{4}{5} + \frac{9}{\boxed{}} = 1\frac{7}{10}$ b) $\frac{11}{12} - \frac{\boxed{}}{5} = \frac{19}{60}$

[   ] 2 marks

Total: [   ] /71 marks

85

Synonyms and antonyms

- Recognise how synonyms and antonyms are related

Synonyms

Synonyms are words with the same or very similar meanings. The right choice of word can make your writing more interesting and avoid repetition.

Example

Word	Synonyms
big	huge enormous vast massive
food	fare meal grub refreshment

> **Remember**
>
> There is often more than one word you can use to say the same thing.

> **Tip**
>
> Use a thesaurus to find synonyms for words.

It is important to choose a word with the right strength of meaning for your writing. To make sure you choose a word correctly, use a dictionary along with a thesaurus to check its exact meaning.

Example

Try Café Pluto

The <u>food</u> in this new café is simply delicious. If you want healthy, tasty <u>refreshment</u>, Café Pluto is the place to go. The <u>fare</u> is served in a vibrant room and is ranked as some of the best <u>grub</u> in town.

Try <u>meals</u> that are out of this world at Café Pluto!

> The food in Café Pluto is referred to five times but the word 'food' is only used once, with synonyms replacing it on every other occasion.

Antonyms

Antonyms are words with opposite meanings.

Example

Word	Antonym
big	small
joyful	miserable
bright	dull

> **Tip**
>
> Dictionaries sometimes give synonyms and antonyms for the words you look up.

Antonyms are sometimes used in texts to show the contrast between different ideas or feelings.

Example

Dull clouds gathered overhead but they could not darken the bright mood of the party.

> The word 'dull' and its antonym 'bright' are both used in the same sentence to highlight the contrast between the weather and the party.

> **Key words**
>
> - synonym
> - antonym

Challenge 1

1. For each highlighted word, tick the **two** synonyms.

   a) **small**   large ☐   slight ☐   mouse ☐   tiny ☐   quiet ☐

   b) **run**   walk ☐   trot ☐   jog ☐   crawl ☐   stroll ☐

   c) **angry**   furious ☐   miserable ☐   disappointed ☐   enraged ☐   upset ☐

   d) **work**   sit ☐   stand ☐   toil ☐   strive ☐   leave ☐

   8 marks

Challenge 2

1. Write **two** antonyms for each given word.

   a) dark   _____   _____

   b) crazy   _____   _____

   c) wet   _____   _____

   d) laugh   _____   _____

   e) sit   _____   _____

   f) tall   _____   _____

   12 marks

Challenge 3

1. Choose a synonym to replace the underlined word in each sentence.

   a) They lived in a **strange** house.   _____

   b) The enemies **looked** at each other.   _____

   c) Samir **walked** slowly to school.   _____

   d) The river was **cold**.   _____

   e) Chloe's bedroom was always **untidy**.   _____

   f) The professor was a very **clever** man.   _____

   6 marks

2. Use each given word, and an antonym of that word, to show a contrast between two nouns in a sentence.

   a) hard

   _____

   _____

   b) hot

   _____

   _____

   4 marks

Total: ☐ /30 marks

Had a go ☐   **Getting there** ☐   **Got it!** ☐

The active and passive voices

- Recognise the active voice and the passive voice
- Use the active and passive voice to present information

What do active and passive mean?

In most writing, the **active voice** is used. This means that the **subject** of the sentence is carrying out the action and the **object** is being acted upon.

Example

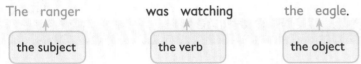

The ranger   was watching   the eagle.

| the subject | the verb | the object |

In the **passive voice**, the subject of the sentence is being acted upon (or having something done to it).

Example

The eagle   was watched.

| the subject | the verb |

The subject from the active sentence (the ranger) may be added to the end of this sentence, preceded by the word 'by'.

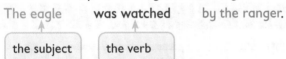

The eagle   was watched   by the ranger.

| the subject | the verb |

Using the passive voice in writing can add interest by varying the sentence structures. It is also very useful if:

- the person doing something is unknown
- the person doing something is being kept from the reader for the time being, for example if you are writing a mystery story.
- the person who did something is not really relevant (and you want the focus to be on what happened rather than who did it).

Example

Active: Somebody **had left** the stolen goods **by the bridge**.

Passive: The stolen goods **had been left** by the bridge.

Active: The well-known thief **had stolen** many precious items **during the night**.

Passive: Many precious items **had been stolen** during the night.

Active: Thousands of people **built** the *Titanic* between 1909 and 1912.

Passive: The *Titanic* **was built** between 1909 and 1912.

The person is unknown so this is better in the passive voice.

The thief's identity is being kept from the reader for now so this works better in the passive voice.

The people who did the building are not relevant for this particular detail so it works better in the passive voice.

Using a combination of active and passive sentences in your writing will help to make it interesting.

Key words

- active voice
- subject
- object
- passive voice

1. Complete each pair of sentences in the past tense with the correct version of the given verb.

a) **bake**

The bakers _____ the bread in the village bakery. (**active**)

The bread _____ in the village bakery. (**passive**)

b) **teach**

Jack _____ Jemima how to play chess. (**active**)

Jemima _____ how to play chess. (**passive**)

c) **fly**

The pilot _____ the plane high in the sky. (**active**)

The plane _____ high in the sky. (**passive**)

d) **drive**

I _____ my new car carefully out of the showroom. (**active**)

My new car _____ carefully out of the showroom. (**passive**)

8 marks

1. Label the sentences about an alien as **active** or **passive**.

a) The alien flew to Earth. _____

b) The alien was transported by a spaceship. _____

c) The alien was watched by some people. _____

d) The alien ran back to the spaceship. _____

e) The spaceship pointed to the sky. _____

f) The spaceship was controlled by the alien. _____

6 marks

1. Write an active sentence and a passive sentence about a chase involving a dog and a cat.

Indicate the subject and verb in each sentence.

_____

_____

_____

_____

_____

_____

6 marks

Total: [ ] /20 marks

| Had a go | | Getting there | | Got it! | |

89

The perfect tense form of verbs

- Use the perfect tense form of verbs to mark relationships of time and cause

The perfect form

The **simple past tense** reports something that happened in the past, e.g.

– We went on holiday.

– I drove the car.

– I finished my lunch.

– I read my new book.

The perfect form is different because it implies a link to another action or event.

The perfect form of a **verb** is used to show that an action has been completed. The words 'have' or 'had' are used along with the verb to show this.

> **Remember**
>
> The ending of many verbs changes for the past tense.

Present perfect

The **present perfect** is used to show a past action that is related to the present. Usually it has happened recently. The action is relevant but the exact time it happened is not.

In the present perfect tense, the word '**have**' is used with the **past participle** of the main verb.

Example

– We have been on holiday.

– I have driven the car.

– I have finished my lunch.

– I have read my new book.

> Present tense of the verb 'to have' and past participle of the main verb.

This tells the reader that we have been on holiday, I have driven the car, I have finished my lunch, and I have read my new book – probably very recently.

Past perfect

The **past perfect** is used to show a past action that happened before another action in the past.

In the past perfect tense, the word '**had**' is used with the past participle of the main verb.

Example

– We had been on holiday, then Mimi got poorly.

> Past tense of the verb 'to have' (had) and past participle of the main verb.

This relates the action of going on holiday to the past, and before another event (Mimi getting poorly).

– I had driven the car but then decided I didn't like it.

This relates the action of driving the car to the past, and before deciding I didn't like it.

– I had finished my lunch before I went out to play.

This relates the action of finishing lunch to the past before going out to play.

– I had read my new book so I bought another.

This relates the action of reading my book to the past, before buying another one.

> **Key words**
>
> - verb
> - present perfect
> - past participle
> - past perfect

1. Complete each pair of sentences with the correct verb.

    a) She _____ created a herb garden. (**present perfect**)

        She _____ created a herb garden before she went home. (**past perfect**)

    b) They _____ decorated the living room. (**present perfect**)

        They _____ decorated the living room before they moved house. (**past perfect**)

    c) I _____ received a new bike. (**present perfect**)

        I _____ received a new bike when I last saw you. (**past perfect**)

    6 marks

1. Label the sentences as **past perfect** or **present perfect**.

    a) We have walked all the way. _____

    b) He had studied well before his exams. _____

    c) I have listened to classical music all my life. _____

    d) I had been feeling unwell all night. _____

    4 marks

1. Change each example below into the present perfect form.

    a) They had played football.

        _____

    b) I had showered.

        _____

    c) He had bought a new shirt.

        _____

    d) She had walked a long way.

        _____

    4 marks

2. Change each example below into the past perfect form.

    a) They have danced to the music.

        _____

    b) We have swum in the sea.

        _____

    c) You have written a story.

        _____

    d) It has rained all day.

        _____

    4 marks

Total: ☐ / 18 marks

Had a go ☐   **Getting there** ☐   **Got it!** ☐

The subjunctive form

- Recognise and use the subjunctive form of a verb

The subjunctive

The **subjunctive** form of a verb is a feature of **formal** writing and speech.

It can also be used to show things such as wishes, demands, hopes or possibility – things that should or could happen.

In most cases the **infinitive form** (basic form) of the verb is used, e.g. write, join, run, drink.

Example

The councillor insisted that he **present** the award. ◄ | *presents* becomes *present* |

She requests that he **join** the gym club. ◄ | *joins* becomes *join* |

The doctor suggested he **run** twice each week. ◄ | *runs* becomes *run* |

It was recommended that she **drink** plenty of water. ◄ | *drinks* becomes *drink* |

In the subjunctive form, the final 's' is removed from the verb.

The verb 'to be' in the subjunctive form

The verb 'to be' behaves differently when used in the subjunctive form:

Present tense of 'to be'	Present subjunctive of 'to be'	Past tense of 'to be'	Past subjunctive of 'to be'
I am	I be	I was	I were
You are	You be	You were	You were
He/She/It is	He/She/It be	He/She/It was	He/She/It were
We are	We be	We were	We were
You are	You be	You were	You were
They are	They be	They were	They were

Example

I wish **I were** able to go skiing. ◄ | *I was* becomes *I were* |

He asked that **they be** informed within the hour.

| *they are* becomes *they be* |

The subjunctive is often used in a subordinate clause.

Example

If they were to go on holiday this year, it would be a surprise.

The subjunctive form is used a lot less nowadays, but you should still know how to use it in your writing and be able to recognise it when reading.

Challenge 1

1. Rewrite each sentence with the underlined verb in the subjunctive form.

   a) If I **was** you, I would try again.

   _____

   b) Dad asked that she **washes** the car.

   _____

   c) It was requested that he **finishes** his homework.

   _____

   d) The officer instructed that the suspects **are** taken to the station.

   _____

   4 marks

Challenge 2

1. Add the subjunctive form of the given verb to complete each sentence.

   a) **to be**   It is important that they _____ at the meeting.

   b) **to take**   The nurse recommended that he _____ a week off.

   c) **to be**   If she _____ well enough, she would visit.

   d) **to wear**   It is imperative that every pupil _____ a school uniform.

   4 marks

2. Underline the verbs in the subjunctive form in the following sentences.

   a) The accountant recommended that she put her money in a bank account.

   b) The robber demanded that the clerk hand over the money.

   c) The police insisted that the main witness write a statement.

   d) They requested that all other people present be questioned.

   4 marks

Challenge 3

1. Rewrite the following sentences in a formal manner using the subjunctive.

   > I wish I was going on the trip with the others. Mr Jones requested that the pupils are at school by 8am and advised that they are picked up at 4pm. If I was going, I would make sure I was there very early.

   _____

   _____

   _____

   _____

   _____

   _____

   5 marks

Total: ☐ / 17 marks

Had a go ☐   **Getting there** ☐   **Got it!** ☐

Using the hyphen

- Use the hyphen correctly with prefixes
- Use the hyphen appropriately to avoid ambiguity

Using the hyphen with prefixes

Most **prefixes** are simply added to the beginning of a word. However, in some cases a **hyphen** is added between the prefix and the **root word**.

Example

- After the prefix 'self', e.g.
  – self-respect
  – self-assessment
- After the prefix 'ex', e.g.
  – ex-player
  – ex-member
- After the prefix 'anti', e.g.
  – anti-clockwise
  – anti-bacterial
- When used with a **proper noun**, e.g.
  – un-British
  – pro-European
- To separate identical vowels, e.g.
  – re-enter
  – re-examine
- To avoid confusion, e.g.
  – re-sent
  – re-cover

> Note that it is sometimes acceptable to leave out the hyphen if the two vowels next to each other are 'o', e.g. cooperate, coordinate.

> Re-sent means something has been sent again; resent means to feel bitter about something.
> Re-cover means to cover something again; recover means to get better.

> **Remember**
>
> Make sure you know what the prefix means before using it.

> **Tip**
>
> If you are unsure whether or not to use a hyphen with a prefix, it is usually acceptable to use one.

Using the hyphen to avoid ambiguity

Sometimes the meaning of a phrase is not clear and so a hyphen is needed to remove any ambiguity (confusion).

Example

Look at the difference that the hyphen makes in these two otherwise identical phrases:

- a man eating tiger
- a man-eating tiger

> The first version could be interpreted as a tiger being eaten by a man. The use of the hyphen in the second version clarifies that it is a tiger that eats people.

Look at the difference that the hyphen makes in these two otherwise identical phrases:

- foreign sales manager
- foreign-sales manager

> The first version could be interpreted as a foreign person who is a sales manager. The use of the hyphen in the second version clarifies that it is a manager of foreign sales.

> **Key words**
>
> - prefix
> - hyphen
> - root word
> - proper noun

Challenge 1

1. Circle the words which must have a hyphen after the prefix. Rewrite them correctly on the line below.

illegal   **im**possible   **pro**American   **ex**husband

revisit   **re**evaluate   **self**aware   **un**grateful

_____

_____

4 marks

Challenge 2

1. Write 'yes' or 'no' after each sentence below to indicate whether or not the hyphen is used correctly.

    a)   They had an old-blue car in the garage.   _____

    b)   She is the ex-manager of the largest store in town.   _____

    c)   You were very in-considerate pushing in the line.   _____

    d)   I saw a crop-spraying aeroplane.   _____

4 marks

2. Add hyphens to make sure each sentence has its given meaning.

    a)   *a bike not used much*   She had a little used bike.

    b)   *cousins who are aged two*   We have two year old cousins.

    c)   *a shark that eats people*   They saw the man eating shark.

    d)   *bugs that destroy flowers*   We spotted the flower destroying bugs.

4 marks

Challenge 3

1. Use a dictionary to help you explain (and write sentences to demonstrate) when a hyphen should and should not be used in the word **repress**.

    _____

    _____

    _____

    _____

2 marks

2. Rewrite these sentences so that the hyphen is used correctly. You may need to remove hyphens as well as add them.

    a)   There are eight ninety year old trees in the big-forest.

    _____

    b)   His friend's exwife has just bought a beautiful new-home.

    _____

    c)   It wasn't possible to-reenter the museum once we had left.

    _____

    d)   She loved going waterskiing when she went on her summer-holidays.

    _____

8 marks

Total: ☐ /22 marks

Had a go ☐   **Getting there** ☐   **Got it!** ☐

Semi-colons

- Use the semi-colon correctly in writing to separate clauses and to separate items in a list

Using the semi-colon to separate clauses

The **semi-colon** is used to separate two independent **main clauses** that are closely related to each other. This means that the clauses should have the same theme.

A semi-colon takes the place of a **conjunction** between the two clauses, so no conjunction is required.

Example

The fishing boat returned and the seagulls arrived with it.

| main clause | conjunction | main clause |

In the sentence above, the two main clauses are related – the seagulls arrived with the boat when it returned.

The conjunction ('and') can be removed and replaced with a semi-colon:

The fishing boat returned; the seagulls arrived with it.

| main clause | semi-colon | main clause |

Using semi-colons is usually down to personal choice but it can have an impact on the reader.

Example

Compare these two sentences:

Lena spent hours trying on clothes, but she could not decide what to wear.

Lena spent hours trying on clothes; she could not decide what to wear.

Both of these sentences are grammatically correct but the sentence using the semi-colon gives more of a sense of why Lena spent hours trying on clothes.

Using the semi-colon in a list

The semi-colon is also used to separate items in a list when the items in the list are more than two or three words, or when one or more of the items contains commas.

Example

On holiday last year, we visited my grandparents in Spain; went on a sightseeing tour of Barcelona; went horse-riding; spent time on the beach and tried lots of local food.

> The items in the list are quite long so they are separated by semi-colons to make them clear.

We met people from all over the world including: Aberdeen, Scotland; Tampa, Florida; Lisbon, Portugal and Jaipur, India.

> The items in the list contain commas so they are separated by semi-colons to make them clear.

Remember

A main clause makes sense on its own.

Tip

Two main clauses can be joined by a conjunction or a semi-colon but make sure there is a clear relationship between each clause.

Key words

- semi-colon
- main clause
- conjunction

Challenge 1

1. Write 'yes' or 'no' after each sentence to indicate whether the semi-colon has been used correctly.

   a) We went to the supermarket and; we bought everything imaginable. _____

   b) The storm blew in from the sea; a rough night lay ahead. _____

   c) Jack had a fantastic model boat; it was raining. _____

   d) The climb was treacherous; concentration was vital. _____

   4 marks

2. Insert a semi-colon in the correct place in each sentence.

   a) The horse hurt its leg again it was still weak from the last injury.

   b) Mum is getting a new car her old car keeps breaking down.

   c) The two sisters are tall in fact they are both taller than their big brother.

   d) Billy likes dance classes at school he has great balance and strength.

   4 marks

Challenge 2

1. Indicate where a semi-colon could be placed in each sentence by putting a line through the word that could be removed and adding the semi-colon.

   a) They sat at a table overlooking the bay and it was a fabulous view.

   b) The Queen waved from the carriage and her loyal subjects cheered.

   c) We spent half the day in the library but we could not find the book we wanted.

   d) There were lots of people singing although I did not join in with my awful voice.

   4 marks

2. Insert a semi-colon in the correct place in each sentence.

   a) Maddie was hoping to visit a number of places on her trip: Barcelona, Spain Lisbon, Portugal Berlin, Germany Paris, France and Venice, Italy.

   b) I had so much to do at the weekend including tidying my bedroom doing all my homework meeting my friends at the cinema going to a football match with my dad taking my sister to her dance class and helping with the gardening.

   2 marks

Challenge 3

1. In the opening line of his famous book, *A Tale of Two Cities*, Charles Dickens wrote:

   It was the best of times; it was the worst of times.

   He could have used a full-stop instead of a semi-colon. What effect do you think the semi-colon has on this sentence?

   _____

   _____

   1 mark

2. Write a sentence containing semi-colons to separate items of three or more words in a list.

   _____

   _____

   _____

   1 mark

   Total: [ ] / 16 marks

   Had a go [ ]   **Getting there** [ ]   **Got it!** [ ]

Dashes

- Use dashes correctly in writing – for parenthesis, to add emphasis, and to express a range between numbers

When to use the dash

The **dash** can be used in different ways. It should not be confused with the **hyphen**, which is shorter.

Using dashes for parenthesis

Just as a pair of brackets and a pair of commas can be used to indicate additional information (**parenthesis**), so can a pair of dashes.

The sentence should still make sense as a main clause if the parenthesis is removed.

Example

The boy (my cousin) is a great juggler.

> A pair of brackets or commas can be used to indicate parenthesis in the same way as a pair of dashes.

The boy, who is actually my cousin, is a great juggler.

The boy – my funny and skilful cousin – is a great juggler.

The juggler – my favourite circus act – received a standing ovation.

The audience – now clapping and cheering – had been mesmerised.

Using a single dash to add emphasis

A single dash can be used to emphasise information or to add information to the clause before it.

Example

She was soon in the lead – she was so fast.

There was only one thing on her mind – winning.

She raised her head and there it was – the finish line.

Using the dash between numbers

A dash can be used to express a range between numbers. If you are writing about a period of time or a range of possibilities between two numbers, use a dash.

Example

The PE lesson is from 10:30–11:30am.

The bikes can easily reach speeds of 30–40 miles per hour.

For homework we have to read pages 32–87 of the book.

In the examples above, the dash effectively replaces the word 'to' or 'until'.

Tip

The dash is longer than the hyphen:

– ◀ dash

- ◀ hyphen

Remember

Parenthesis is used to add further information to a sentence. A pair of dashes can be used to indicate parenthesis.

Key words

- dash
- hyphen
- parenthesis

Challenge 1

1. Tick the sentences that use the dash correctly.

   a) My dad – who lives on a canal boat is lots of fun. ☐

   b) The engine – old and noisy – still worked. ☐

   c) It was a lovely gesture – making cakes – and eating them. ☐

   d) There were three stars in that team – all fast and skilful. ☐

   ☐ 1 mark

Challenge 2

1. Rewrite each sentence using a dash or dashes.

   a) They read about a journey around the world from 1889 to 1895.

   _____

   _____

   b) The headteacher stood waiting for that golden moment silence.

   _____

   _____

   c) My mum's necklace the one with the silver locket is very precious.

   _____

   _____

   d) The buses run from 0800 to 1500, between my village and town.

   _____

   _____

   ☐ 4 marks

Challenge 3

1. Use dashes when writing sentences for each given idea.

   a) Write a sentence saying that the explorers wanted just one thing and that thing was water.

   _____

   _____

   b) Write a sentence to say that the Labrador won the dog show, with parenthesis explaining that it was Marley's friend's dog.

   _____

   _____

   c) Write a sentence saying that Harry went on holiday to Spain every year from 2005 to 2014.

   _____

   _____

   ☐ 3 marks

Total: ☐ /8 marks

Had a go ☐   **Getting there** ☐   **Got it!** ☐

99

Colons and bullet points

- Use colons correctly to introduce lists, examples and speech
- Use a colon correctly to separate clauses
- Use bullet points correctly to create lists

Colons

Colons can be used to introduce a list, introduce an example, introduce speech and introduce numbered points or **bullet points**.

Using a colon to introduce a list

Sometimes a list appears in a sentence with no introduction. However, the colon can be used to make it clear that a list is about to appear in the writing.

Example

Maddy, Duncan, Ella and Joe went to the park. ← A list with no introduction.

The children who went to the park were: Maddy, Duncan, Ella and Joe. ← A list with a colon to introduce it.

Using a colon to separate two clauses

A colon can be used to separate two independent clauses where the second clarifies the first. When using a colon in a sentence between two connected clauses, each clause must contain a **subject** and a **verb**.

Example

Horses are intelligent: Dan's horse recognises the noise made by his car. ← This sentence uses a colon to add an example that backs up the first clause.

Using a colon to introduce speech

Colons are used to introduce speech in a playscript.

Example

Juliet: At what o'clock to-morrow shall I send to thee? ← The colon after the character's name shows who is speaking.

Romeo: At the hour of nine.

Using a colon to introduce bullet points

A colon can be used to introduce bullet points.

Example

Learning to play tennis requires:
- reasonable fitness
- co-ordination
- training

Bullet points are used to make items in a list easier to read and locate in a text.

With bullet points, remember:
- to use a colon before the bullet points start
- that each bullet point usually contains a single idea
- that the bullet points can start with upper-case or lower-case letters
- there should be consistency (lower-case or upper-case)
- that bullet points may not be full sentences so full stops may not be required

Challenge 1

1. Tick the sentences that use the colon correctly.

    a) Steph was now on the school council: she had won the class vote. ☐

    b) It was the car they had wanted: Sam went to school. ☐

    c) They had cakes: oranges, apples, sandwiches. ☐

    d) Her favourite authors are: Wilson, Pullman, Horowitz and Rowling. ☐

    ☐ 1 mark

Challenge 2

1. Indicate where colons could be used in each example below.

    a) She did several events throwing, jumping, running and cycling.

    b) His guitar was beautiful the craftsmanship was of the highest quality.

    c) Every year we visit four places the beach, the pier, the fairground and the beachside café.

    d) They reached the summit of the mountain it was due to their excellent training plans.

    ☐ 4 marks

Challenge 3

1. Read this sentence.

    > Their camping list included a tent, sleeping bags, inflatable beds, a water carrier and a gas stove.

    a) Rewrite the sentence using a colon.

    _____

    _____

    ☐ 1 mark

    b) Rewrite the sentence using bullet points.

    _____

    _____

    _____

    _____

    _____

    _____

    ☐ 2 marks

2. Look at the bullet points below. Rewrite them as a list introduced by a colon in a sentence.

    Key features of Kyle's racing bike:
    *   Lightweight saddle
    *   Narrow tyres
    *   Aerodynamic shape
    *   Special paint

    _____

    ☐ 2 marks

Total: ☐ / 10 marks

Had a go ☐   **Getting there** ☐   **Got it!** ☐

Progress test 5

1. **Read the extract.**

> It was a lovely morning as they slipped into the icy pool. With a shiver they watched an eagle soar overhead. A stiff breeze was starting to blow and after their swim they longed for the warmth of the fire.

In the text, find a synonym for each word below.

a) **beautiful** _____

b) **cold** _____

c) **fly** _____

d) **strong** _____

e) **heat** _____

5 marks

2. Indicate where dashes could be used in each example below.

a) It was an incredible story quite inspirational.

b) The school library opens from 12:30 to 3:00 each day.

c) Beside the tree the one with the treehouse we found a fossil.

d) Queen Victoria lived from 1819 to 1901.

4 marks

3. Write a sentence using each given word. Use a dictionary to help you, if needed.

a) descent

_____

_____

b) dissent

_____

_____

2 marks

4. **Check the spelling of each word below.**

Place a tick next to each word that is spelt correctly. Then write the correct spelling for each incorrect word on the lines below. Use a dictionary to help you if needed.

a) percieve ☐   b) believe ☐

c) protein ☐   d) ceiling ☐

e) caffeine ☐   f) beleif ☐

g) sieze ☐   h) conciet ☐

_____

_____

8 marks

5. Label the sentences as **past perfect** or **present perfect**.

   a) They have cooked our lunch. _____

   b) We had prepared everything before we left. _____

   c) They have cleaned the house. _____

   d) I had watched the sunrise before breakfast. _____

4 marks

6. For each underlined word, circle the two synonyms.

   a) **funny**   loud   hilarious   joke   amusing   laugh

   b) **rich**   wealthy   empty   affluent   good   strive

   c) **tall**   big   length   towering   strange   sky

   d) **sad**   tear   sniff   unhappy   bad   tragic

8 marks

7. Add the subjunctive form of the given verb to complete each sentence.

   a) to listen   It is vital that she _____ to her teacher.

   b) to attempt   The coach recommended that he _____ a new distance.

   c) to be   If he _____ taller, he would not fit in the den.

   d) to be   It is important that I _____ there on time.

4 marks

8. Insert a semi-colon in the correct place in each sentence.

   a) It was an easy journey the sea was calm.

   b) Their cake was judged to be the best they were great bakers.

   c) Nobody could have guessed the ending it was a total surprise.

   d) Eating in the restaurant was delightful every dish was a masterpiece.

4 marks

9. Rewrite the following information using bullet points.

   She decided that, in London, she wanted to visit Trafalgar Square, Buckingham Palace, Big Ben, the Tower of London and the London Eye.

   _____

   _____

   _____

   _____

   _____

   _____

2 marks

10. **Write sentences that show examples of each of the following types of figurative language.**

a) Onomatopoeia: _____

_____

b) Simile: _____

_____

c) Metaphor: _____

_____

d) Personification: _____

_____

e) Alliteration: _____

_____

f) Hyperbole: _____

_____

6 marks

11. **Read the extract.**

> Finally, it was time to go home. The afternoon had lasted forever. Grabbing his coat and bag, Henry dashed outside into the torrential rain. He sprinted out of the school grounds quickly, heading for home. Today was the day that his mum was picking up their new pet. He threw his coat over his head to shield him from the rain as he ran. Dirty water from the deep puddles splashed his trousers.
>
> He rounded the corner and half skipped up to his front door. Already, he could hear little squeals coming from inside the house. Taking a deep breath, he excitedly opened the door.

a) What do you think might happen next? _____

_____

b) Which words tell you that Henry was in a rush? _____

_____

_____

c) Find and copy the example of hyperbole from the text.

_____

d) Give three examples of adverbs from this extract.

_____

e) Give three examples of adjectives from this extract.

_____

5 marks

12. **Read this sentence.**

> They needed to sort out lots of things for the party including booking a venue; finding a DJ; ordering the food; making a cake; buying the decorations and sending out invitations.

Rewrite the sentence using a colon and semi-colons.

_____

_____

_____

_____

13. **Write a bullet-pointed list of six objects that could be found in a kitchen.**

_____

_____

_____

_____

_____

_____

_____

14. **Circle the correct homophone or near-homophone in each sentence.**

a)   They should have listened to the **advise / advice**.

b)   Water was scarce in the scorching **desert / dessert**.

c)   Jen chose the shorter **root / route** back to the town.

d)   It was very **quite / quiet** in the house.

15. **Some of these sentences are written in the active voice and some are written in the passive voice. Rewrite each sentence using the opposite voice.**

a)   The book was created by Shivi.

_____

b)   He hadn't eaten the cake yet.

_____

c)   I made a phone call last night to my friend.

_____

d)   The boys broke the window yesterday.

_____

e)   The fence was built by my neighbour.

_____

Total: [   ] / 65 marks

Converting units of measurement

- Know how to convert between metric units using decimal notation to three decimal places
- Convert between miles and kilometres

Converting metric units to three decimal places

Learning the relationship between metric units will make converting units much quicker. You need to know how to use **decimal notation** to convert to three **decimal places**.

To convert a larger unit to a smaller unit you need to **multiply**.

Example

Convert 0.25 litres to centilitres.

$\quad$ 1 l = 100 cl

0.25 × 100 = 25

Answer: 0.25 l = 25 cl

Convert 3.525 kilometres to metres.

$\quad$ 1 km = 1,000 m

3.525 × 1,000 = 3,525

Answer: 3.525 km = 3,525 m

To convert a smaller unit to a larger unit you need to **divide**.

Example

Convert 0.75 millimetres to centimetres.

$\quad$ 10 mm = 1 cm

0.75 ÷ 10 = 0.075

Answer: 0.75 mm = 0.075 cm

Convert 10,575 millilitres to litres.

$\quad$ 1,000 ml = 1 l

10,575 ÷ 1,000 = 10.575

Answer: 10,575 ml = 10.575 l

> **Remember**
>
> To multiply numbers by 10, 100 or 1,000, move the digits one place, two places or three places to the left. When dividing, move the digits one place, two places or three places to the right. This may involve moving the digits across a **decimal point**.

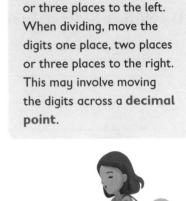

Miles and kilometres

Imperial measures are an older system of measures that were used for many years before **metric measures** were adopted.

A frequently used and useful conversion is changing miles to kilometres and vice versa.

1 mile is approximately 1.6 km.

Rather than multiplying or dividing by 1.6, it is easier to use fractions:

$1.6 = 1\frac{6}{10} = 1\frac{3}{5} = \frac{8}{5}$

- To convert miles into kilometres, find $\frac{8}{5}$ of the number of miles: divide by 5 and multiply by 8
- To convert kilometres into miles, find $\frac{5}{8}$ of the number of kilometres: divide by 8 and multiply by 5

Example

Convert 15 miles to km.

$\quad$ 15 ÷ 5 = 3 and 3 × 8 = 24

Answer: 15 miles is approximately **24 km**

Convert 32 km to miles.

$\quad$ 32 ÷ 8 = 4 and 4 × 5 = 20

Answer: 32 km is approximately **20 miles**

> **Remember**
>
> There are more kilometres for miles so dividing by 5 and multiplying by 8 will give a larger answer; when changing kilometres to miles, the number will be less, so divide by 8 and multiply by 5

> **Key words**
>
> - decimal notation
> - decimal place
> - decimal point
> - imperial measures
> - metric measures

Challenge 1

1. Convert these larger units to smaller units.

   a) 3.5 km = [ ] m   b) 4.2 kg = [ ] g   c) 10.5 litres = [ ] ml

   3 marks

2. Convert these smaller units to larger units.

   a) 225 cm = [ ] m   b) 3,500 ml = [ ] litres   c) 125 g = [ ] kg

   3 marks

PS 3. Cobi sees a sign in France that says the distance he must drive is 64 kilometres.
   Approximately how far is this in miles?

   _____

   1 mark

PS 4. The distance from Chen's hotel to the beach is 15 miles.
   Approximately how far is this in kilometres?

   _____

   1 mark

Challenge 2

1. Convert these larger units to smaller units.

   a) 10.75 km = [ ] m   b) 4.02 kg = [ ] g   c) 1.005 litres = [ ] ml

   3 marks

2. Convert these smaller units to larger units.

   a) 25 cm = [ ] m   b) 30.5 cl = [ ] litres   c) 5 g = [ ] kg

   3 marks

PS 3. The distance between Calais and Paris is 300 kilometres.
   Approximately how far is this in miles?

   _____

   1 mark

PS 4. The distance from Land's End to John O'Groats is 877 miles.
   Approximately how far is this in kilometres?

   _____

   1 mark

Challenge 3

1. Convert these larger units to smaller units.

   a) 0.025 km = [ ] m   b) 10.025 kg = [ ] g   c) 12.15 litres = [ ] ml

   3 marks

2. Convert these smaller units to larger units.

   a) 125 m = [ ] km   b) 5 ml = [ ] litres   c) 15,275 g = [ ] kg

   3 marks

PS 3. Molly knows that it is 321 km from Calais to her holiday campsite. She has driven 105 miles.
   Approximately how many more kilometres does she have to drive?

   _____

   1 mark

PS 4. Neema flies from London to New York. It is 3,493 miles. The pilot announces that there
   are 1,000 km left to fly.
   Approximately how many miles has the aeroplane flown?

   _____

   1 mark

   Total: [ ] **/24 marks**

   Had a go [ ]   **Getting there** [ ]   **Got it!** [ ]

Perimeter and area

- Recognise that shapes with the same areas can have different perimeters and vice versa
- Calculate the area of parallelograms and triangles

Areas and perimeters of rectangles

Rectangles can have the same **area** but different **perimeters**, or the same perimeter but different areas.

A rectangle with an area of 24 cm² could have these and other perimeters:	A rectangle with a perimeter of 30 cm could have these and other areas:
28 cm (length 12 cm, width 2 cm)	14 cm² (length 14 cm, width 1 cm)
22 cm (length 8 cm, width 3 cm)	36 cm² (length 12 cm, width 3 cm)
20 cm (length 6 cm, width 4 cm)	50 cm² (length 10 cm, width 5 cm)

> **Remember**
>
> Use the correct units:
> - length for perimeters, e.g. centimetres or metres
> - squares for areas, e.g. **square centimetres** (cm²) or **square metres** (m²).

Example

Joe has 20 lengths of fencing. Each length is 2 metres long.

He uses them to make a rectangular enclosure with the largest possible area.

What is the largest possible area?

There are 20 lengths of fencing to form the perimeter. As a rectangle they could be rectangles arranged as 9 × 1, 8 × 2, 7 × 3, 6 × 4 or 5 × 5.

Arranging the lengths as 5 × 5 gives the largest area: each length is 2 metres long, making each side of the enclosure 10 metres.

This gives an area of **100 m²**.

Areas of parallelograms and triangles

The area of a rectangle is the length multiplied by the width.

In the diagrams, b (**base**) is equivalent to the length of a rectangle and h (**height**) is equivalent to the width of a rectangle.

To find the area of a parallelogram:

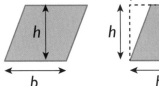

> By moving the shaded triangle on the parallelogram it is possible to make a rectangle.
>
> Area of a parallelogram = $b \times h$
>
> A parallelogram with a base of 6 cm and height of 4 cm has an area of (6 × 4 =) 24 cm².

To find the area of a triangle:

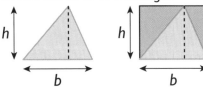

> A triangle is half of a rectangle. The area of a triangle will also be half the area of a rectangle.
>
> Area of a triangle = $(b \times h) \div 2 = \dfrac{b \times h}{2}$
>
> A triangle with a base of 8 cm and a height of 5 cm has an area of $(\dfrac{8 \times 5}{2} =)$ 20 cm².

> **Key words**
>
> - area
> - perimeter
> - square centimetres/metres
> - base
> - height

Challenge 1

1. Dan arranges some centimetre squares to make a rectangle with a perimeter of 20 cm.

Which other rectangles could Dan make using centimetre squares that have a perimeter of 20 cm?

Give the length and width of four rectangles.

_____

_____

4 marks

2. Find the area of a parallelogram with a base of 12 cm and a height of 5 cm. _____

1 mark

3. Find the area of a triangle with a base of 12 cm and a height of 5 cm. _____

1 mark

Challenge 2

1. Give the length and width (whole numbers) of four different rectangles with a perimeter of 24 cm.

_____

_____

4 marks

2. Give the length and width (whole numbers) of four different rectangles with an area of 36 cm^2.

_____

_____

4 marks

3. Find the area of a parallelogram with a base of 25 cm and a height of 12 cm. _____

1 mark

4. Find the area of a triangle with a base of 50 cm and a height of 20 cm. _____

1 mark

Challenge 3

PS 1. Find the length of a square where the perimeter and area have the same numeric value.

☐ cm

1 mark

2. Find the area of a parallelogram with a base of 8.5 cm and a height of 3 cm. _____

1 mark

3. Find the area of a triangle with a base of 10.5 cm and a height of 6 cm. _____

1 mark

PS 4. Using whole numbers only, find:

a) the largest perimeter for a rectangle with an area of 48 cm^2. _____

b) the smallest area for a rectangle with a perimeter of 48 cm. _____

c) the height of a triangle with a base of 12 cm and an area of 12 cm^2. _____

d) the base of a parallelogram with a height of 20 cm and an area of 600 cm^2. _____

4 marks

Total: ☐ /23 marks

Had a go ☐   **Getting there** ☐   **Got it!** ☐

Volume

- Calculate volumes of cubes and cuboids

Volumes of cubes and cuboids

The **volume** of a cube or cuboid is the amount of space it takes up. Volume is measured using cubes. These can be **cubic centimetres** or **cubic metres**, or any unit of measure of length.

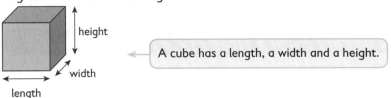

height

width

length

A cube has a length, a width and a height.

Example

This cuboid is 5 cm long, 4 cm wide and 3 cm high.

There is a row of five shaded cubes along the length of the top of the cuboid:

5 cm³

There are four similar rows on the top of the cuboid:

5 cm³ × 4 = 20 cm³

There are three similar layers of the cuboid:

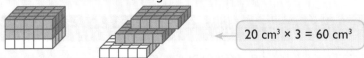

20 cm³ × 3 = 60 cm³

The volume is: number of cubes in a row × number of rows in a layer × number of layers.

As a formula: $V = l \times w \times h$

For this cuboid: $5 \times 4 \times 3 = 20 \times 3 = 60$

Answer: Volume is 60 cm³.

Example

The area of the shaded face is 36 cm² and the length of the cuboid is 12 cm.

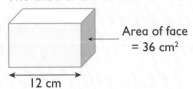

Area of face
= 36 cm²

12 cm

What is the volume of the cuboid?

The area of the shaded face has been found by multiplying the width by the height: 36 cm².

To find the volume, the final part of the calculation is to multiply the area of the end face by the length.

$36 \times 12 = 432$

Answer: Volume is 432 cm³.

Challenge 1

1. Find the volume of these cuboids.

   a) 8 cm, 12 cm, 20 cm ☐ cm³

   b) 10 cm, 15 cm, 30 cm ☐ cm³

   2 marks

2. Complete this table giving the volume of cuboids with the given measurements:

	Length	Width	Height	Volume
a)	8 cm	8 cm	4 cm	_____
b)	6 cm	9 cm	3 cm	_____
c)	10 cm	5 cm	7 cm	_____

	Length	Width	Height	Volume
d)	12 cm	4 cm	5 cm	_____
e)	10 cm	10 cm	20 cm	_____
f)	9 cm	9 cm	9 cm	_____

6 marks

Challenge 2

1. What is the volume of cubes that have sides of:

   a) 6 cm? _____   b) 8 cm? _____

   2 marks

PS 2. Jack is building a cuboid 8 cm long, 4 cm wide and 3 cm high using centimetre cubes.

   He starts building the cuboid but runs out of centimetre cubes.
   This drawing shows how much Jack has completed.

   How many more centimetre cubes does he need?

   _____

   1 mark

PS 3. The area of the base of a cuboid is 72 cm² and the height is 5 cm.

   What is the volume of the cuboid? _____

   1 mark

Challenge 3

PS 1. Manisha builds a cuboid using centimetre cubes. The cuboid is 8 cm long, 5 cm wide and 6 cm high.
   She can also use the same number of cubes to make a different cuboid.

   What could the length, width and height of Manisha's second cuboid be?

   _____

   1 mark

PS 2. Find the volume of a cuboid 0.5 m long, 5 cm wide and 5 cm high.

   ☐ cm³

   1 mark

PS 3. The area of face A on this cuboid is 90 cm²; the area of face B is 36 cm².

   Face B is square.

   What is the volume of the cuboid?

   ☐ cm³

   1 mark

   Total: ☐ **/ 15 marks**

Had a go ☐   **Getting there** ☐   **Got it!** ☐

2-D and 3-D shapes

- Compare, classify and describe 2-D shapes including circles, and 3-D shapes
- Draw 2-D shapes and use nets of 3-D shapes

2-D shapes

You need an understanding of the properties of **2-D** shapes.

Example

Here are five numbered shapes drawn on a square grid.

Which shape has one pair of **parallel** sides, two **acute** angles and one **line of symmetry**?

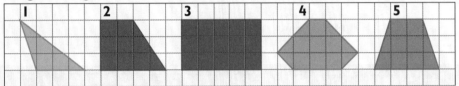

Shape 1 has two acute angles, but no parallel sides and no line of symmetry.

Shape 2 has one pair of parallel sides, but only one acute angle and no line of symmetry.

Shape 3 has two pairs of parallel sides and two lines of symmetry, but no acute angles.

Shape 4 has one line of symmetry and three pairs of parallel sides but has no acute angles.

Shape 5 has one pair of parallel sides, two acute angles and one line of symmetry.

Answer: Shape 5

> **Remember**
>
> Learn and recall the properties of 2-D shapes that were covered in earlier years.

> See page 114 for angles.

Circles

The dotted lines in each diagram show the name for that part of the circle.

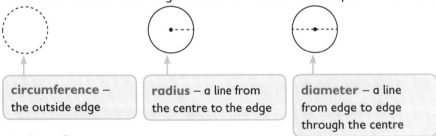

circumference – the outside edge

radius – a line from the centre to the edge

diameter – a line from edge to edge through the centre

3-D shapes

3-D shapes have faces. When these faces are 'opened up' they form the **net** of the 3-D shape.

Example

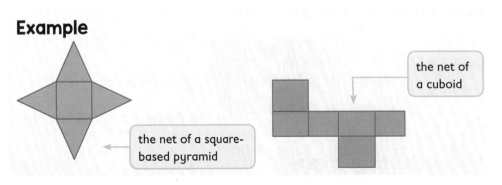

the net of a cuboid

the net of a square-based pyramid

> **Key words**
>
> - 2-D
> - parallel
> - acute angle
> - line of symmetry
> - circumference
> - radius
> - diameter
> - 3-D
> - net

Challenge 1

1. This rectangle is drawn on a square grid. A triangle is drawn inside the rectangle which creates four triangles inside the rectangle.

   a) Which triangles are right-angled triangles? _____

   b) Which triangle is an isosceles triangle? _____

   c) Which triangle has an obtuse angle? _____

   3 marks

2. Circle the name of the straight line which runs from the centre of a circle to the outside edge.

   circumference   **radius**   **diameter**   **perimeter**   **base**

   1 mark

3. For which 3-D shape is this net?

   _____

   1 mark

Challenge 2

1. Which two shapes have at least one set of parallel lines, one line of symmetry and at least one obtuse angle?

   _____

   1 mark

2. These lengths are the diameters of different circles. What is the radius of each?

   a) 23 cm _____   b) 16.5 cm _____

   2 marks

3. Circle the net that is **not** a net of a cube.

   A   B   C   D   E

   1 mark

Challenge 3

1. Circle the word that **cannot** correctly complete the sentence:

   A square is also a _____.

   rectangle   **rhombus**   **parallelogram**   **quadrilateral**   **trapezium**

   1 mark

2. Four circles fit exactly into a rectangle. Each circle has a radius of 2.5 cm.

   What is the length and width of the rectangle?

   _____

   1 mark

3. A cube has one black circle.

   This is the net of the cube.
   Write B on the base of the net.

   1 mark

   Total: ⬚ **/ 12 marks**

   Had a go ⬚   **Getting there** ⬚   **Got it!** ⬚

Angles

- Find unknown angles in triangles, quadrilaterals and regular polygons
- Find unknown angles at a point, on a straight line or when vertically opposite

Angles in 2-D shapes

The **angles** in a triangle always total **180°**. Knowing this will also help you to find the total number of degrees in the angles of a quadrilateral, because all quadrilaterals can be divided into two triangles.

Angles in every triangle total 180° so the angles in every quadrilateral total (180 × 2 =) 360°.

These facts help to find missing angles.

Example

In the triangle:

17° + 42° + A = 180°

59° + A = 180°

A = 180° − 59° = **121°**

In the quadrilateral:

61° + 114° + 31° + B = 360°

206° + B = 360°

B = 360° − 206° = **154°**

In **regular polygons**, the size of the **interior** (inside) **angles** can be calculated.

- All regular polygons can be divided into triangles.
- A regular pentagon can be divided into a **minimum** of three triangles with no **intersecting** internal lines, so the total number of degrees in a regular pentagon is 540° (180° (degrees in 1 triangle) × 3).
- Each internal angle must be 108° (540° ÷ 5 (number of internal angles)).
- The interior angle for any regular polygon can be calculated in a similar way.

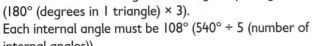
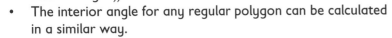

Angles and lines

Angles around a point total 360°, and angles on a straight line total 180°. Vertically opposite angles are equal. Knowing these facts means you can work out missing angles.

Example

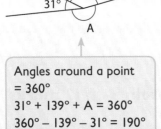 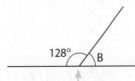 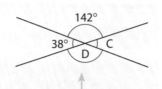

Angles around a point = 360°

31° + 139° + A = 360°

360° − 139° − 31° = 190°

A = 190°

Angles on a straight line = 180°

128° + B = 180°

180° − 128° = 52°

B = 52°

The angle 38° and angle C are vertically opposite and therefore equal.

C = 38°

D = 142°

Challenge 1

1. Find the missing angles.

   a)

   b)

   c)

   d)

   e)

   5 marks

Challenge 2

1. Find the missing angles in the shapes in these tables.

Triangles		
a) 109°	36°	_____
b) 48°	77°	_____
c) 58°	67°	_____

Quadrilaterals			
d) 43°	52°	107°	_____
e) 68°	83°	158°	_____
f) 93°	102°	119°	_____

   6 marks

PS 2. In a classroom, some children sit at a table that has a top the shape of a regular hexagon.

   What is the size of the angle at each corner?

   1 mark

Challenge 3

1. Find the missing angles.

   a) Two identical parallelograms make this hexagon.

   b) An equilateral triangle and a square share a common side.

   2 marks

PS 2. An isosceles triangle has an angle that is 66°

   What could one of the other different angles be? Give two possible answers.

   _____

   2 marks

PS 3. A ship is sailing north. It turns to sail south-east.

   What is the angle of the turn?

   _____

   1 mark

   Total: ☐ **/ 17 marks**

   Had a go ☐   **Getting there** ☐   **Got it!** ☐

Coordinate grids

- Describe positions on a full coordinate grid

Positions on a full coordinate grid

A full **coordinate grid** uses four **quadrants** separated by the **x-axis** and the **y-axis**. The 1st quadrant is the top right quadrant and the other quadrants are numbered anti-clockwise.

Negative numbers as well as positive numbers are used on the axes.

The coordinates of a point on a coordinate grid are always written using the x-coordinate followed by the y-coordinate, separated by a comma and within brackets.

Remember

The coordinates of any point on a coordinate grid are written in brackets using the x-coordinate followed by the y-coordinate.

Example

A rectangle has been drawn on the coordinate grid below.

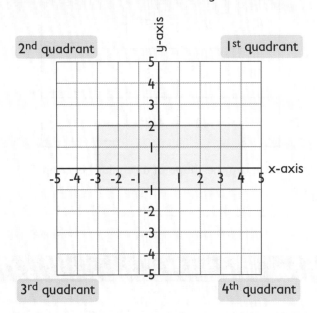

The coordinates of this rectangle are (−3, 2), (4, 2), (−3, −1) and (4, −1).

You may come across a question that uses coordinates without a grid. You should still be able to work out the answer.

Example

A line is drawn between two points on a coordinate grid. The points have the coordinates (2, 3) and (−4, −3).

What are the coordinates of a point halfway along the line?

The x-coordinates are 2 and −4 ← Halfway between these two coordinates is −1

The y-coordinates are 3 and −3 ← Halfway between these two coordinates is 0

Answer: The halfway point on the line is **(−1, 0)**.

Key words

- coordinate grid
- quadrant
- x-axis
- y-axis

Challenge 1

1. A trapezium is drawn on the coordinate grid.

    What are the coordinates of the vertices of the trapezium?

    _____

     1 mark

2. A straight line is drawn from (−4, 2) to (4, −2).

    What are the coordinates of the point halfway along the line?

    _____

     1 mark

3. Draw a square on the coordinate grid with vertices at the coordinates (0, −1), (−2, −2), (−1, −4) and (1, −3).

     1 mark

Challenge 2

1. The three black dots show three of the vertices of a square.

    a) What are their coordinates?

    _____

    b) What are the coordinates of the fourth corner of the square?

    _____

     2 marks

2. Three vertices of a rectangle are (2, 5), (4, 3) and (3, 2).

    a) Plot these coordinates on the grid.

    b) Complete and draw the rectangle.

     2 marks

3. These points are drawn on a coordinate grid so that they make a straight line: (−4, 4), (−2, 3), (0, 2), (2, 1).

    If the points are continued, what will be the next point drawn?

    _____

     1 mark

Challenge 3

1. The three black dots show three of the vertices of a parallelogram.

    Find three possible answers for the fourth vertex.

    _____

     3 marks

2. Three vertices of a kite are (3, 4), (1, 3) and (5, 3).

    What could the coordinates of the fourth corner be?

    _____

     1 mark

3. Three of the coordinates of the vertices of a square are (−1, 5), (−4, 2) and (2, 2).

    a) What are the fourth coordinates of the square?

    _____

    b) What are the coordinates of the centre of the square?

    _____

     2 marks

Total: / 14 marks

Had a go ☐   **Getting there** ☐   **Got it!** ☐

Reflection and translation

- Draw and translate shapes on the coordinate plane and reflect them in the axes

Translating shapes

The **translation** of a shape is a sideways or up-and-down movement of the shape. The shape does not change size or orientation.

Example

A red rectangle is drawn on the **coordinate grid**. If the rectangle is translated 5 squares left and 6 squares up, it will move to the position of the blue rectangle.

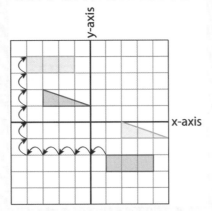

Describe the translation of the red triangle to the position of the blue triangle.

The triangle has been translated 5 squares right and 2 squares down.

Reflecting shapes

The **reflection** of a shape is when the shape is 'flipped' over a 'mirror line' or 'line of reflection'.

Example

A red shape is drawn on the coordinate grid. If the shape is reflected in the y-axis, then it will move to the position of the blue shape. In this case the y-axis is the mirror line.

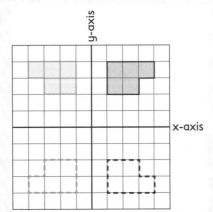

Reflect the red shape in the x-axis and then in the y-axis.

The red dotted shape shows the position after the first reflection. The blue dotted shape shows the position after the second reflection.

Challenge 1

1. a) Translate Rectangle A, 4 squares left and 4 squares down.

    Draw the rectangle in its new position.

    b) Translate Triangle B, 6 squares right and 3 squares up.

    Draw the triangle in its new position.

    2 marks

2. Describe the translation of Square C to Square D.

    _____

    1 mark

3. Reflect:

    a) Rectangle A in the x-axis.

    b) Triangle B in the y-axis.

    2 marks

Challenge 2

1. Describe the translation of:

    a) Rectangle B to Rectangle A.

    _____

    b) Rectangle C to Rectangle A.

    _____

    2 marks

2. Looking at Rectangles A to D, which rectangles show a translation of:

    a) 3 squares left, 1 square up? _____

    _____

    b) 1 square right, 3 squares up? _____

    _____

    2 marks

3. Reflect:

    a) Trapezium E in the x-axis.   b) Pentagon F in the y-axis.

    2 marks

Challenge 3

1. There are three trapeziums A, B and C. Describe the translation of:

    a) Trapezium A to Trapezium C.

    _____

    b) Trapezium C to Trapezium B.

    _____

    2 marks

2. Reflect Quadrilateral D in the x-axis and the y-axis on the grid.

    1 mark

3. Parallelogram E is reflected in the y-axis. What will the coordinates of the reflected parallelogram be?

    _____

    1 mark

    Total: ☐ / 15 marks

Had a go ☐   **Getting there** ☐   **Got it!** ☐

Pie charts and line graphs

- Interpret and construct pie charts and use them to solve problems
- Interpret and construct line graphs and use them to solve problems

Pie charts

A **pie chart** divides a circle into sectors to show the proportions of data. If the total of the data is known, the number of each data item can be calculated or estimated.

Example

Children in a year group were given a choice of visits to support their work in school. The results were displayed in a pie chart.

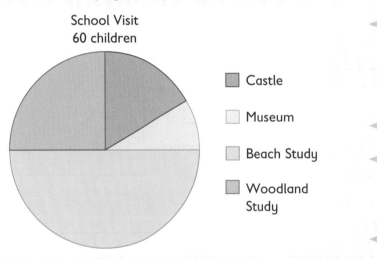

School Visit
60 children

- Castle
- Museum
- Beach Study
- Woodland Study

> The number of children taking part is shown under the title.

> The largest sector shows those who wanted to take part in the Beach Study. This sector is half of the pie chart, so this must be 30 children (60 ÷ 2).

> The sector for the Woodland Study is 90°. This sector is one quarter, so must show 15 children (60 ÷ 4).

> Calculation means 15 children must have wanted to visit the Castle or the Museum (60 – 30 – 15).

Pie charts are often constructed using the angles of the sector at the centre. If the angle of the Museum sector was 30°, this must be one-twelfth as there are 360° in a full turn ($\frac{30}{360} = \frac{1}{12}$).

Line graphs

A **line graph** gives **continuous data**, usually over a period of time.

Example

This line graph shows the temperature in a classroom between 8:00 a.m. and 4:00 p.m. The temperature has been taken every two hours and the points fixed on the graph. The line joins these points and shows the **trend** of the temperature.

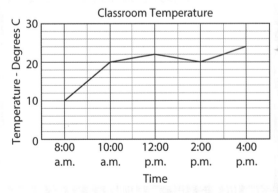

Classroom Temperature

Remember

On a line graph, between the fixed points, the temperature shown is the best estimate.

> Read the graph by following vertical and horizontal lines.
> The temperature at 2:00 p.m. is 20 °C.
> The temperature at 9:00 a.m. is estimated to be 15 °C.

Key words

- pie chart
- line graph
- continuous data
- trend

Use the pie chart and the line graph to answer the questions in the Challenges.

The pie chart shows where guests staying at a hotel come from.

Hotel Guests
100 guests

☐ UK
☐ Ireland
☐ France
☐ Germany

The line graph shows the distance from home a car has travelled on a journey.

Car Journey

Distance in miles

160
140
120
100
80
60
40
20
0

1:00 p.m. 1:30 p.m. 2:00 p.m. 2:30 p.m. 3:00 p.m. 3:30 p.m.

Time

Challenge 1

1. Use the pie chart to:

   a) work out the number of guests who live in the UK. ☐

   b) estimate the number of guests who live in Ireland. ☐

   ☐ 2 marks

2. Use the line graph to:

   a) estimate the total distance travelled. _____

   b) estimate how long it took to drive the first 40 miles. _____

   ☐ 2 marks

Challenge 2

1. On the pie chart, the same number of guests live in Ireland as in France.

   There are twice as many guests from France as Germany.

   How many guests come from Germany? ☐

   ☐ 1 mark

2. Use the line graph to:

   a) calculate how far the car travelled between 2:30 p.m. and 3:00 p.m.

   _____

   b) give the minimum time the car stopped for during the journey.

   _____

   ☐ 2 marks

Challenge 3

1. On the pie chart, how many more guests come from the UK as from Ireland?

   ☐

   ☐ 1 mark

2. 20 more guests from Norway arrive at the hotel. This data is added to the pie chart.
   What is the size of the angle of the sector to show the guests from Norway?

   ☐

   ☐ 1 mark

3. Using the line graph, explain why the journey may not have begun at 1:00 p.m.

   _____

   _____

   _____

   ☐ 1 mark

Total: ☐ / 10 marks

Had a go ☐   Getting there ☐   Got it! ☐

121

Mean as an average

- Calculate and interpret the mean as an average

The mean

The **mean** is one type of **average**. It involves taking a set of **numerical data**, totalling it and 'sharing' it out equally.

Other types of average are the **median** and the **mode**.

Example

Sally has 12 sweets, Meena has 9 sweets and Yana has 3 sweets.

They agree that they should each have an equal number of sweets.

The three girls put their sweets into one bag and share them out equally.

There are (12 + 9 + 3 =) 24 sweets in total.

When they share the sweets out, each girl gets (24 ÷ 3 =) 8 sweets.

The mean is **8**

> The mean of 12, 9 and 3 is:
> 12 + 9 + 3 = 24
> 24 ÷ 3 = 8

Example

Find the mean of 25, 36, 47, 55 and 62

Step 1:   Add the numbers: 25 + 36 + 47 + 55 + 62 = 225

Step 2:   Divide by the number of numbers

225 ÷ 5 = 45   ← There are five numbers.

Answer: The mean is **45**

You may come across problems that require an understanding of the **revised mean**, which is when another number is added to the set.

Example

The mean of 6 numbers is 32

A seventh number, 46, is added to the set of numbers.

What is the revised mean?

If the mean of the numbers is 32 and there are 6 numbers, the total of the numbers is (32 × 6 =) 192

If 46 is added to the total of the numbers, then the new total will be (192 + 46 =) 238

To find the mean of 7 numbers with a total of 238, divide the total by the number of numbers (7):

238 ÷ 7 = 34

Answer: The revised mean is **34**

Challenge 1

1. Find the mean of these numbers: **49, 61, 117, 261** ☐ ☐ 1 mark

PS 2. Keeley completes a mental arithmetic exercise every day for a week at school. Her results for the week were:

15, 15, 18, 17, 20

What was her mean result? ☐ ☐ 1 mark

PS 3. Ben has a stall in the market. His daily takings for the 6 days he is open during one week are:

£126   £98   £118   £83   £108   £121

What are his mean daily takings for those 6 days? ☐ ☐ 1 mark

PS 4. Two consecutive numbers have a mean of 13.5

What are the numbers?

☐ and ☐ ☐ 1 mark

Challenge 2

1. Find the mean of these numbers: **45, 87, 32, 27, 10, 36, 22** ☐ ☐ 1 mark

PS 2. Three consecutive numbers have a mean of 156

What are the three numbers?

☐ , ☐ and ☐ ☐ 1 mark

PS 3. Dev buys four books. The prices of the books are **£8.70, £2.30, £3.85 and £6.99**

What is the mean price of the books? ☐ ☐ 1 mark

PS 4. Jenny's dog has four puppies. The mean mass of the puppies is 1,075 g.

The masses of three of the puppies are: **1,050 g, 1,080 g, 1,090 g.**

What is the mass of the fourth puppy? ☐ ☐ 1 mark

Challenge 3

PS 1. Eight numbers have a total of 348. What is the mean of the numbers? ☐ ☐ 1 mark

PS 2. Here is a set of five numbers: **78   56   198   128   ?**

There is one number missing. The mean of the numbers is 105.

What is the missing number? ☐ ☐ 1 mark

PS 3. Kyle works as a gardener. One week his mean daily pay for the first four days is £115.

After the fifth day, his mean daily pay for the five days has increased to £118.

How much was Kyle paid on the fifth day?

☐ ☐ 1 mark

PS 4. Harry buys three books that cost £4.99 each and two books that cost £5.99 each.

What is the mean cost of the books? ☐ ☐ 1 mark

Total: ☐ / 12 marks

Had a go ☐   **Getting there** ☐   **Got it!** ☐

123

Progress test 6

1. Tick the circle that has a dotted line showing the diameter of the circle.

 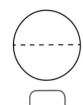 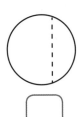

| | | | |

1 mark

2. Convert these measurements to the unit given.

   a) 6.5 kg = _____ g

   b) 7.9 cm = _____ mm

   c) 9.35 m = _____ cm

   d) 3975 m = _____ km

   e) 10,825 ml = _____ litres

   f) 8.025 kg = _____ g

6 marks

3. a) Reflect the triangle in the x-axis.   b) Reflect the quadrilateral in the y-axis.

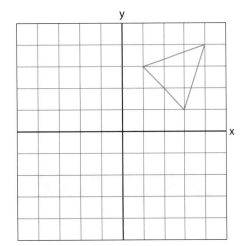 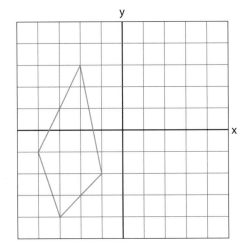

2 marks

4. Calculate the missing angles.

   a)

   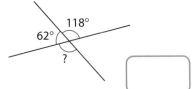

   118°
   62°
   ?

   b)

   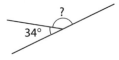

   ?
   34°

   c)

   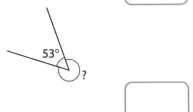

   53°
   ?

   d)

   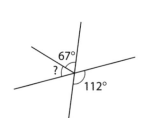

   67°
   ?
   112°

4 marks

124

PS 5. This pie chart shows how Manny spends his money each month.

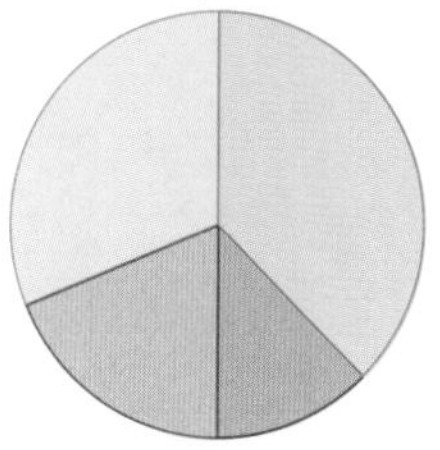

Manny's Spending
£1,600

☐ Rent
☐ Household Bills
☐ Food
☐ Spending Money

a) If Manny spends £200 on his household bills each month, how much does he spend on his rent?

_____

b) Estimate how much spending money Manny has each month.

_____

2 marks

PS 6. Jethro has 36 square tiles. Each tile is a centimetre square. He uses the tiles to make a larger square that measures 6 cm by 6 cm.

a) What is the perimeter of Jethro's larger square? _____

1 mark

b) Jethro re-arranges his 36 tiles into different rectangles.

Find two other perimeters that the other rectangles could have.

_____

2 marks

7. Find the area of these two triangles.

a)

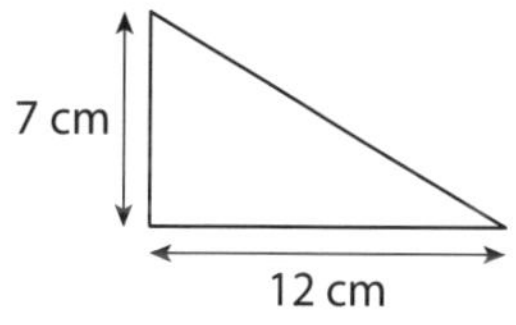

7 cm
12 cm

☐ cm²

b)

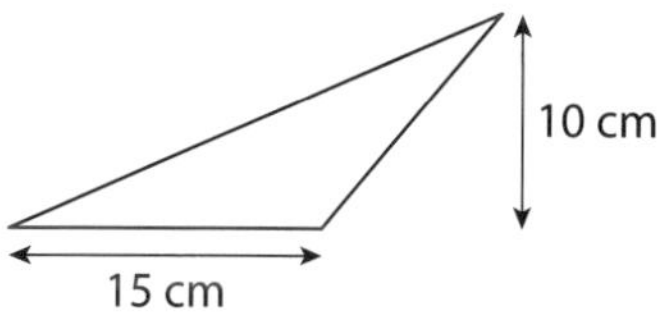

10 cm
15 cm

☐ cm²

c) Find the height of a triangle with an area of 80 cm² and a base of 20 cm.

_____

3 marks

PS 8. Pav drives 60 km.

How many miles is this?

☐

1 mark

9. What is the base of a parallelogram with an area of 125 cm² and a height of 5 cm?

_____

1 mark

125

10. Here are three 3-D shapes.

triangular prism   cuboid   square-based pyramid

a) Which **two** of these shapes both have five faces?

_____

b) Which **two** of these shapes have parallel faces?

_____

PS c) Gus says, "Only the square-based pyramid has at least one face that is square."

Is Gus correct?   Circle   **YES / NO**

Explain your answer. _____

_____

PS d) Parveen says, "Only the cuboid has faces with 2-D shapes that have right angles."

Is Parveen correct?   Circle   **YES / NO**

Explain your answer. _____

_____

4 marks

PS **11. A circus erects a circular tent. It is 35 metres from one side of the tent to the other through the middle of the tent.**
A pole is at the centre of the tent to hold the roof up.

How far is it from the edge of the tent to the pole at the centre?

_____

1 mark

PS **12. Mrs Singh has 8 pupils in her maths group. She gives the pupils a test.**

Two of the pupils score 80%, two of the pupils score 70% and the other four pupils score 60%.

What is the mean score of the pupils in Mrs Singh's maths group?

_____

1 mark

13. Find the area of parallelograms that have:

a) a base of 14 cm and a height of 5 cm. _____

b) a base of 30 cm and a height of 20 cm. _____

2 marks

14. Circle the shape that is **not** the net of a cuboid.

A   B   C   D

1 mark

126

15. a) Translate the triangle 4 squares left and 5 squares up.
Draw the triangle in its new position.

b) Translate the quadrilateral 3 squares right and 2 squares down.
Draw the quadrilateral in its new position.

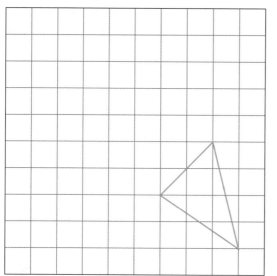

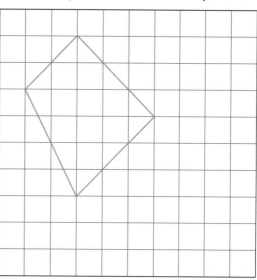

2 marks

16. Find the missing angles in these isosceles triangles.

a)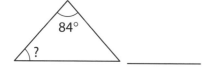

84°

? _____

b)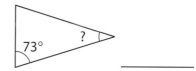

73° ?

_____

2 marks

17. Find the missing angles in these regular shapes.

a)

? _____

b)

? _____

2 marks

18. Jamelia and Jasmine each grow a sunflower. On the first day of each month they record the height of their sunflowers on a line graph.

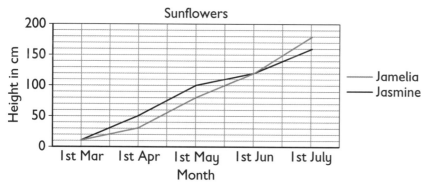

a) Estimate the height of Jasmine's sunflower on June 15th. _____

b) Estimate the difference between the height of the sunflowers on July 1st. _____

2 marks

Total: ☐ /40 marks

127

English mixed questions

1. **Explain the meaning of each prefix and each whole word.**

   a) illegal _____

   _____

   b) misread _____

   _____

   c) disagree _____

   _____

   d) unprepared _____

   _____

   8 marks

2. **Underline each example of onomatopoeia in the text below.**

   > The rattle of wheels on the tracks was followed by the squeal of brakes as the train tried to stop. The chatter of birds paused, as if they knew what was about to happen.

   3 marks

3. **Complete each sentence by adding a suffix to a word selected from the list below.**

   decent   significant   president   dominant

   a) His _____ of the tennis club expired after 3 years.

   b) It was too late by the time they realised the _____ of their actions.

   c) After several years, their _____ of the school athletics tournaments came to an end.

   d) He showed great _____ in sharing his winnings with friends and family.

   4 marks

4. **Circle the correct homophone.**

   a) Lena's bike was heavy because it was made from **steal / steel**.

   b) Mimi took the horse's **reins / reigns** confidently.

   c) At the end of their performance, they all took a **bough / bow**.

   d) The vet told her the cat was **mail / male**.

   e) I have **serial / cereal** for breakfast every day.

   f) He gave an excellent **insight / insite** into the history of the town.

   6 marks

5. **Indicate whether each of the following sentences contains a simile, metaphor or personification.**

   a) They heard a boom, as loud as thunder. _____

   b) Sunlight peeped over the houses and crept along the street. _____

   c) The pond was a mirror reflecting the moonlight. _____

   d) His stomach was a bottomless pit. _____

   e) The engine growled but the tyres squealed with joy as the race started. _____

   f) Her blue eyes sparkled like the ocean. _____

   6 marks

6. **Read the two passages below. One passage is from a school newsletter, and the other is from a Year 6 pupil's diary.**

> **A**   We had a great time on the museum trip. Everyone loved the mechanical T-Rex family but they weren't all that scary. The dinosaur bones and models were dead boring after though.
>
> We had lunch in the museum café. The food was yummy but it was a bit of a rip-off.
>
> It's worth a visit to the museum because there are loads of things to see and do.

> **B**   The museum trip was a great success. The pupils were fascinated by the mechanical Tyrannosaurus Rex family, and did not appear to find it too frightening. It was hard for the rest of the dinosaur exhibition to live up to the high standard of the T-Rex family.
>
> Lunch was taken in the excellent museum café. Although not cheap, the quality of the food was high.
>
> We would recommend a visit to the museum to see the exhibits and activities for yourself.

a)   Write which passage is which and state whether it is **formal** or **informal**.

School newsletter _____   Formal or informal? _____

Diary entry _____   Formal or informal? _____

4 marks

b)   Choose a word or phrase from the first paragraph of each passage which shows that it is formal or informal.

Passage A: _____

_____

Passage B: _____

_____

2 marks

c)   Compare the formal and informal versions of the second paragraph of each passage. Explain two differences between them.

_____

_____

_____

_____

_____

_____

2 marks

7. Write two antonyms for each given word.

    a) wild   _____   _____

    b) wonderful   _____   _____

    c) love   _____   _____

    d) whisper   _____   _____

8 marks

8. Read the poem then answer the questions.

> **The Journey**
> The beginning, a stick, a stream,
> Tossed from rock to rock,
> Then drifting like a proud ship,
> In an elegant river, wider and deeper,
> With bigger sticks, branches and real boats,
> And plastic bags and bottles, floating human shame,
> As the water empties into the sea,
> Surrounded by small fish,
> Then caught in a large fishing net,
> The end? Or a new beginning?

a) Why do you think this poem is called 'The Journey'?

    _____

    _____

b) What simile is used in the poem?

    _____

c) Explain the contrast between the words 'tossed' and 'drifting' (lines 2 and 3).

    _____

    _____

    _____

d) What do you think is meant by the words 'floating human shame'?

    _____

e) Find and copy two examples of alliteration from the poem.

    _____

    _____

    _____

f) Why do you think the poem ends with questions?

    _____

    _____

6 marks

9. **Read the passage below, then answer the questions.**

The River Amazon, at over 4,000 miles, is the second longest river in the world. It flows through dense rainforests, teeming with life in South America. As it does so, this incredible river passes through several countries including Peru, Ecuador and Brazil. From its source (its starting point) in the Andes mountains, it makes its way to the Brazilian coast and into the Atlantic Ocean. No other river in the world carries as much water as the Amazon, and in the wet season parts of the river can reach 120 miles wide.

a) Find and copy the key words or phrases from the passage for each question below.

What? _____

Where from? _____

_____

Where to? _____

_____

3 marks

b) Précis the passage, making sure you cover all the main points.

_____

_____

_____

_____

_____

1 mark

10. **Change each sentence into the present perfect form.**

a) We had cooked a lovely meal.

_____

b) She had found the hidden path.

_____

2 marks

11. **Change the verb in each sentence to the subjunctive form.**

a) They requested that the decorator **paints** the office white. _____

b) Mum suggested that Dan **cleans** his bike. _____

c) The shopkeeper instructed that the deliveries **are** put in the van. _____

d) I don't know what would happen if I **was** to write them a letter. _____

4 marks

12. **Which of these words should have a hyphen after the prefix? Circle them and then rewrite them correctly below.**

misdiagnose   **ex**president   **un**happy   **ir**relevant

selfconscious   **re**enter   **pro**European   **im**mature

_____

4 marks

13. **Place a tick next to the sentences where dashes have been used correctly.**

   a)   I saw the man – from the television in a car.   ☐

   b)   My neighbour – Mrs Brown from school – has a dog.   ☐

   c)   The bread – freshly baked this morning – was delicious.   ☐

   d)   She is always polite and well-behaved – a delightful girl in fact.   ☐

   ☐ 1 mark

14. **Indicate where colons could be used in each example below.**

   a)   They needed the following ingredients eggs, butter, flour, sugar and chocolate.

   b)   It was a beautiful view the mountains reflected in the surface of the lake.

   c)   The team for the match is as follows Devon, Jess, Molly, Khalid, Zac and Elsie.

   d)   An incredible surprise awaited them Grandma had come to visit from Australia.

   ☐ 4 marks

15. **Write two English words that are derived from the following words.**

   a)   *Script* (from Latin meaning to *write*)

   _____

   b)   *Chrono* (from Greek meaning *time*)

   _____

   c)   *Aqu* (from Latin meaning *water*)

   _____

   d)   *Geo* (from Latin meaning *earth*)

   _____

   ☐ 8 marks

16. a)   **Read the text below and emphasise three key words or phrases by underlining them.**

   The Panama Canal
   The 48-mile long canal cuts through the country of Panama, joining the Atlantic Ocean with the Pacific Ocean. Before it opened, shipping would have to sail around Cape Horn through hazardous seas in a journey which took up to 5 months longer.

   ☐ 3 marks

   b)   Explain your choices of key words or phrases.

   _____

   _____

   ☐ 1 mark

132

c) The text is an extract from a page about the world's longest canals.

Briefly describe the sort of content that could be placed in a fact box for the page.

_____

_____

_____

1 mark

17. Some of these sentences are written in the active voice and some are written in the passive voice. Rewrite each sentence using the opposite voice.

a) The best team won the football match.

_____

b) He sold his games console.

_____

c) A speeding ticket was issued by the police officer.

_____

d) Emma smashed Mum's vase.

_____

e) Syed packed the suitcases.

_____

5 marks

18. Explain how the comma changes the meaning in the two sentences below.

A   Are you going to visit Mike?

B   Are you going to visit, Mike?

_____

_____

_____

_____

1 mark

19. Read the sentences. Tick the one that is definite.

I should go home now. ☐

I might go to the shops. ☐

I could go to the cinema later. ☐

I will go to visit my friend. ☐

1 mark

133

20. Read the text below and then answer the questions.

> The sky was getting darker and I pulled the collar of my thin jacket up and walked faster. My legs felt heavy and it was difficult pushing against the aggressive, forceful wind. Since I'd arrived here, it had turned bitterly cold and my fingers, without gloves, felt like icicles.
>
> I turned the corner by the park and saw movement out of the corner of my eye. I spun round quickly to look, my eyes darting around like tiny fish in a tank, but I couldn't see anything. I hurried on, looking and listening, now so aware of my unfamiliar surroundings – a quiet, tired part of town that seemed to be clinging on to me, refusing to let me go.

a) Give two examples of similes from the text.

_____

_____

b) Give two examples of adverbs from the text.

_____

c) Give two examples of adjectives from the text.

_____

d) Give an example of personification from the text.

_____

_____

e) Give an example of alliteration from the text.

_____

8 marks

21. Look at the underlined words. Write the correct word for each.

a) In the distance, they **herd** a cuckoo. _____

b) Jess asked the teacher for some **advise**. _____

c) The old toy soldier was made from **led**. _____

d) She was not **aloud** on the lawn when it was wet. _____

4 marks

22. Rewrite this extract using at least four cohesive devices to make it read better.

> Billy rushed into the classroom. He sat down at his desk. He took off his coat and took out his books. He sat back relieved. Mr Jewson strode into the room. He had a stern look on his face. The class went silent.

_____

_____

_____

_____

_____

4 marks

23. Read this poem and then answer the questions.

Pretty swallow, once again
    Come and pass me in the rain.
    Pretty swallow, why so shy?
    Pass again my window by.

Pretty little swallow, fly
    Village doors and windows by,
    Whisking o'er the garden pales
    Where the blackbird finds the snails;

On that low thatched cottage stop,
    In the sooty chimney pop,
    Where thy wife and family
    Every evening wait for thee.

a)   Which word rhymes with 'shy'?

_____

b)   What rhyme scheme does this poem use? Tick the correct answer.

ABAB   ☐

AABB   ☐

ABCB   ☐

ABBA   ☐

c)   In the second verse, what does the swallow fly over?

_____

d)   Which other type of bird is mentioned in the poem?

_____

e)   What do you think the last two lines mean?

_____

_____

_____

5 marks

Total: ☐ / 109 marks

Maths mixed questions

1. a) 149 + 152 = _____

    b) 45 × 4 = _____

    c) 640 ÷ 8 = _____

    d) 1000 – 123 = _____

2. **Circle the net of the triangular prism.**

    A   **B**   **C**   **D**   **E**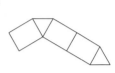

PS 3. **There are two levels of seats at a concert hall. There are 2,752 seats on the lower level and 1,867 seats on the upper level. At a concert, there are 128 empty seats on the lower level and 86 empty seats on the upper level.**

    How many seats were taken? _____

PS 4. **This table shows the temperatures in UK cities on January 1st.**

City	Belfast	Brighton	Cardiff	Glasgow	Liverpool	Norwich
Temp.	–2 °C	4 °C	3 °C	–4 °C	–1 °C	2 °C

    a) What is the difference in temperature in Cardiff and Liverpool? _____

    b) Which two cities have a difference in temperature of 7 °C?

    _____

5. **Simplify these fractions to their lowest terms.**

    a) $\frac{16}{20}$ = ☐   b) $\frac{16}{24}$ = ☐   c) $\frac{15}{25}$ = ☐

6. **Calculate:**

    500,000 – 50,000 = _____

PS 7. **At a party, Meena puts 5 pizzas out on the table. The fractions show how much of each pizza was left.**

    Tick the pizza that had most eaten.

    $\frac{1}{3}$ $\frac{1}{4}$ $\frac{3}{8}$ $\frac{5}{12}$ $\frac{7}{24}$

    ☐   ☐   ☐   ☐   ☐

8. a) 6,800 ÷ 20 = _____

    b) 6,143 × 26 = _____

9. a) Translate the hexagon 5 squares left and 2 squares up.

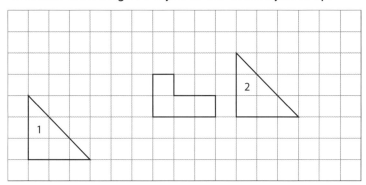

b) Describe the translation of Triangle 1 to Triangle 2.

_____

2 marks

PS 10. An estate agent sells three houses in one week. Two of the houses sell for £275,000 each and another house sells for £320,000.

What is the mean sale price of the houses? _____

1 mark

PS 11. Joe buys some clothes in a sale. He buys:

• an £80 coat that is reduced in price by 20%

• a pair of £60 trainers that are reduced by 25%

How much does he save altogether?

_____

1 mark

PS 12. These shapes represent numbers.

◯ + ◯ + ◯ + ▢ + ▢ = 52

◯ + ◯ + ◯ + ▢ = 44

Find the value of:

a) ▢ = _____   b) ◯ = _____

2 marks

13. Circle the number where the digit 3 represents thirty thousand.

53,067   1,309,721   752,630   2,439,157   3,074

1 mark

PS 14. Amy sells bunches of roses from her flower stall. People can choose the number of roses in each bunch. Each rose costs £2 and she charges £3 for the display packaging.

Amy uses C for the total cost and r for the number of roses.

Circle the formula Amy can use to work out the cost of a bunch of roses.

C = r + 2 + 3   C = 3r + 2   C = 2(r + 3)   C = 2r + 3   C = 3(r + 2)

1 mark

15. Complete the tables by rounding the numbers.

	Rounded to the nearest 1,000
14,708	
256,005	

	Rounded to the nearest 100,000
1,908,418	
4,960,148	

4 marks

137

16. These two triangles are similar. Find the length of Side A.

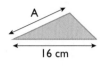 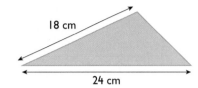

A = ☐ cm

17. Here are some numbers:

5   6   8   11   18   20   26   33

a) Which two numbers are common multiples of 4? ☐ and ☐

b) Which two numbers are factors of 30? ☐ and ☐

c) Which two numbers are prime numbers? ☐ and ☐

18. a) Calculate:

$50 - 25 \times 2 \div 10 + 5^2 =$ ☐

b) Add brackets to make this calculation correct.

$40 + 50 \div 10 + 15 = 42$

PS 19. Polly plans on using centimetre cubes to make a cuboid that is 10 cm long, 8 cm wide and 6 cm tall, but she does not have enough cubes.

She decides to make each measurement half the size and makes that cuboid instead.

a) What is the volume of the cuboid Polly makes?

_____

b) What is the fraction of the actual number of cubes to the planned number?

_____

20. Convert these measures.

a) 7,825 g = _____ kg

b) 4.25 cm = _____ mm

c) 20.125 km = _____ m

d) 12,575 ml = _____ litres

e) 2,575 m = _____ km

PS 21. A factory makes toy cars. The cars are packed in boxes holding 12 cars. The boxes are then packed into packs of 48 boxes for loading onto a lorry.

A lorry can hold 80 packs.

How many cars will it take to fill the lorry?

_____

22. Petra puts these three fractions in order, starting with the smallest.

The numerator of one of the fractions is missing. Add it in.

$$\frac{3}{10} \qquad \frac{\boxed{}}{20} \qquad \frac{2}{5}$$

23. Sam and Dev complete a traffic survey outside their homes for an hour and record the number of vehicles that pass. They record the results in pie charts.

Sam's Traffic Survey
160 vehicles

☐ Bus
☐ Lorry
☐ Van
☐ Car

Dev's Traffic Survey
60 vehicles

☐ Bus
☐ Lorry
☐ Van
☐ Car

a) How many vans passed Sam's house? ☐

b) An equal number of buses and lorries passed Sam's house.

How many buses passed Sam's house? ☐

c) An equal number of buses, lorries and vans passed Dev's house.

How many buses passed Dev's house? ☐

d) How many more cars passed Sam's house than Dev's house? ☐

24. Max has used $\frac{2}{5}$ of a bag of potatoes.

He has enough potatoes left to make three portions of chips.

What fraction of the bag of potatoes is used to make a portion of chips?

25. Complete this table by finding the fraction, decimal and percentage equivalents.

Fraction		Decimal		Percentage
$\frac{1}{5}$	=		=	
	=	0.25	=	
	=		=	80%
$\frac{1}{20}$	=		=	

26. Find the area of these shapes.

a)

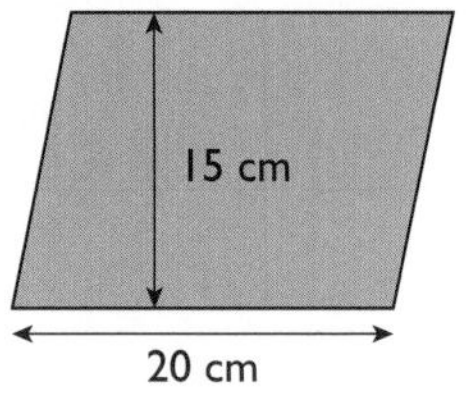

15 cm
20 cm

☐ cm^2

b)

20 cm
30 cm

☐ cm^2

☐ 2 marks

27. Use the square grid to draw a pentagon with three right angles.

☐ 1 mark

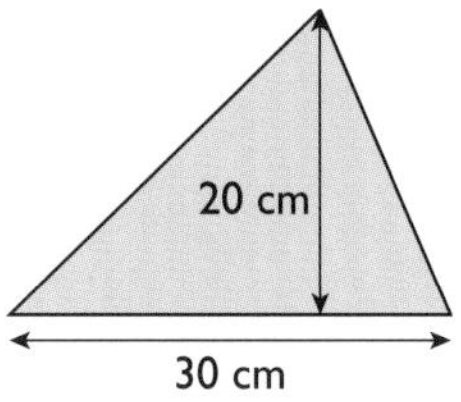

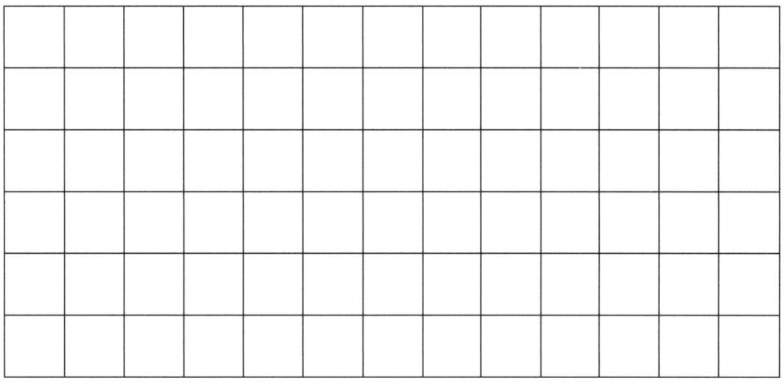

28. Write seven million, sixty-three thousand, four hundred and six in figures.

____

☐ 1 mark

PS **29. Shona takes five parcels to the Post Office. Altogether the parcels have a mass of 11 kg.**

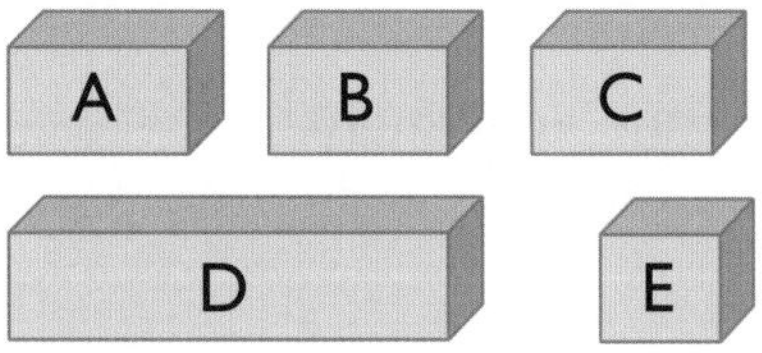

A
B
C
D
E

Parcels A, B and C have the same mass.

Parcel D is twice the mass of Parcel A.

Parcel E is half the mass of Parcel A.

What is the mass of Parcel A?

☐ kg

☐ 1 mark

PS 30. This graph shows the temperature inside and outside a greenhouse.

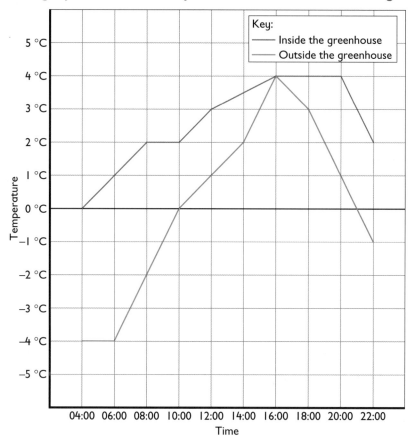

a) What was the temperature inside the greenhouse at 08:00?

_____

b) When did the temperature outside the greenhouse first reach 0 °C?

_____

c) For how long was the outside temperature above 0 °C?

_____

d) Estimate the temperature inside the greenhouse at 11:00.

_____

e) What was the difference between the inside and outside temperatures at 08:00?

_____

5 marks

PS 31. Dot says, "Isosceles triangles can be acute-angled or obtuse-angled triangles but cannot be right-angled triangles."

Is Dot correct?   **YES / NO**

Explain your answer. _____

_____

1 mark

32. Look at the grid.

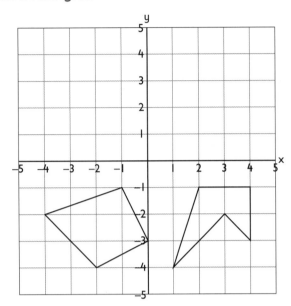

a) What are the coordinates of the pentagon on the grid?

_____

1 mark

b) Reflect the pentagon in the x-axis and then reflect the shape in the y-axis.

2 marks

c) Translate the quadrilateral 4 squares right and 5 squares up.

1 mark

PS **33.** Dave describes a 3-D shape.

He says, "My shape has 6 faces, 10 edges and 6 vertices. Five of the faces are identical isosceles triangles."

What shape is Dave describing?

_____

1 mark

34. Estimate the answers to the calculations by rounding numbers to the nearest ten thousand.

a) 35,920 + 20,387 + 29,632 =   Estimated answer = _____

b) 78,256 − 59,521 =   Estimated answer = _____

2 marks

PS **35.** A machine packs tins of biscuits into boxes of 15 tins.

If there are 2,815 tins of biscuits, how many full boxes will there be?

1 mark

36. Find the missing numbers.

a) 0.7 × _____ = 5.6

b) _____ × 9 = 0.36

c) _____ × 12 = 4.8

3 marks

37. A number (y) is divided by 5 and 15 is subtracted. Circle the expression that shows this calculation.

$15 - \dfrac{5}{y}$ $15 - \dfrac{y}{5}$ $\dfrac{15 - 5}{y}$ $\dfrac{5}{y} - 15$ $\dfrac{y}{5} - 15$

PS 38. The Trans-Siberian Railway crosses Russia. The distance is 9,260 kilometres.

Approximately what is this distance in miles?

_____

39. a) A rectangle is made with centimetre tiles.

It has an area of 48 cm². Its measurements are recorded in this table.

Complete the table with the length and width of three different rectangles that have the same area.

Length	Width	Area
8 cm	6 cm	48 cm²
		48 cm²
		48 cm²
		48 cm²

b) Another rectangle has a perimeter of 22 cm.

Complete the table with the length and width of three different rectangles that have a perimeter of 22 cm.

Length	Width	Perimeter
		22 cm
		22cm
		22 cm

PS 40. Five identical circles are drawn inside a hexagon so that the sides of each just touch.

The perimeter of this hexagon is 120 cm.

What is the radius of one of the circles? ☐ cm

PS 41. x and y stand for positive whole numbers.

What could the values of x and y be in the equation $3x + 2y = 22$?

Find three possible solutions.

If x = _____ , then y = _____

If x = _____ , then y = _____

If x = _____ , then y = _____

Total: ☐ /89 marks

Answers

Page 5
Challenge 1
1. **a)** explain   **b)** sign   **c)** medic   **d)** compose
Challenge 2
1. **a)** mis = incorrect, wrong; heard incorrectly
    b) un = not; not believable
    c) im = not; not possible
    d) over = too much; get too hot/too much heat
    e) bi = two; every two years
    f) aero = air/atmosphere; study of air and space travel.
    g) trans = across/through; plant across
Challenge 3
1. **a)** transport   **b)** prescribe   **c)** excitement
    d) misinformation   **e)** superhuman
2. unbelievable, miscalculated, insufficient, disallowed, discovered, inaudible

Page 7
Challenge 1
1. **a)** F **b)** I **c)** I **d)** F **e)** I **f)** F
Challenge 2
1. **a)** Formal. Examples: A brochure or leaflet, or a report about the place.
    b) Informal. Examples: Letter or postcard to a friend.
Challenge 3
1. Any three ideas showing the difference between the formal and informal language. Examples:

Formal	Informal
several activities;	loads to do;
children and adults;	kids and grown-ups;
participate;	take part;
safety equipment;	safety stuff;
are compulsory;	you have to wear;
these are readily available;	there are loads of them;
keeps queuing to a minimum	don't have to wait long

2. Examples:
    a) I would very much like the job as I think I would be excellent at it.
    b) One man was hitting the other. It was quite a fight.

Page 9
Challenge 1
1. air hissed; splashing water; squawk of a seagull
2. air hissed spitefully; paddles played at splashing
Challenge 2
a) simile
b) metaphor
c) personification
d) simile
e) personification
f) personification
Challenge 3
1. Clear understanding of the differences needed, with examples used from Challenge 2 or other suitable examples given. Examples:
    A simile is when something is compared to something else, e.g. the mouse was as brave as a lion.
    Metaphor is when we say something is something else, e.g. the windmill – a monster on the horizon.
    Personification is when something is given human qualities, e.g. the flowers bowed their heads.

2. laughed their heads off
    so loud and high-pitched it could shatter glass.
    bouncing off the walls with excitement.

Page 11
Challenge 1
1. **a)** silently – to give an idea of peace and calm
    b) One of: blue, daily – the explanation for the chosen word should be that it adds more detail and helps the reader imagine the scene and/or the character better.
Challenge 2
1. **a)** a swamp of treacle
    b) trees lay like fallen soldiers
2. **a)** Answer should acknowledge that these words are used to show the contrast between 'normal' and the 'heavy, sticky and deep mud' that was now faced.
    b) Answer should acknowledge that by showing that the wall was strong, it also shows how powerful the water must have been to whisk it away.
Challenge 3
1. Responses should have a reasonable link to the text. Examples:
    a) He might be a farmer (because it seems that he is in the countryside/he's looking at a herd).
    b) He is upset because the herd is 'far smaller than usual' – animals may have been swept away by the flood.

Page 13
Challenge 1
1. Lines rhyme in pairs – AABB pattern. 'plain' with 'rain', 'rest' with 'west', etc.
2. Most likely answers: sun, breeze
Challenge 2
1. Response should have a reasonable fit with the text. Example: It is about somebody riding away from an enemy/ being chased, making an escape on horseback.
Challenge 3
1. **a)** silently creeping   **b)** graceful white sheet

Page 15
Challenge 1
1. **a)** Response should acknowledge that it was an amazing feat or a difficult time barrier to break.
    b) To list some key information/to make it easier to see some information.
Challenge 2
1. Getting started ✓ Warming up ✓
2. Both fit with a text for a person inspired to start running.
Challenge 3
1. **a)** Yes – because it links to the introduction about Roger Bannister, and it links to inspiration.
    b) No – although it mentions running races, there is no mention in the main text about the Olympics.

Pages 16–19
Progress test 1: English
1. **a)** disappoint**ment**   **b)** **ir**responsible
    c) **dis**appeared   **d)** kind**ness**   **e)** **un**usual
2. **a)** boulders   **b)** briefly
    c) Because she is just an average person but now finds herself as the first person ever on Mars.
    d) The answer should make sense based on what has been read. It could be that there is something there and action ensues, or it could be that her mind is playing tricks on her.

e) The answer should acknowledge that she is tired (no time to relax, long trip) or fed up with the instructions (she sighed, more instructions, no time to relax).

f) 'Large boulders sat proudly' is personification – the small rocks are given human characteristics.
'surrounded by an audience of smaller rocks' is a metaphor/alliteration of the 's' sound.
'like children listening to a great storyteller' is a simile – the small rocks are compared to children.

3. Examples:
   a) enjoyable   b) insensitive   c) medicine
   d) inexplicable   e) prefix or suffix

4. impossible; illegible; decoded; illegal; unusual; unconventional

5. a) I   b) I   c) F   d) F   e) F   f) I

6. a) It is a well-known phrase to represent something mysterious or spooky.
   b) witnessed
   c) The answer should fit with the overall theme and the content of the fact box. Examples: 'Mysteries around the world', 'More mysteries'.
   d) The answer should include that the author is probably sceptical – 'and unsurprisingly, many have not', 'But surely they're not true', 'or not, as the case may be'. Even 'things that go bump in the night' could be seen as poking a bit of fun.

7. a) treat   b) nation   c) cover   d) pass

8. a) simile   b) metaphor or personification
   c) personification   d) simile   e) metaphor

9. so hungry he could eat a horse
   been walking forever
   slower than a snail
   covered about a million miles

10. a) ABCB ✓   b) Personification   c) died

MATHS
Page 21
Challenge 1
1. a) 200,000 or two hundred thousand
   b) 8,000 or eight thousand
   c) 1,000,000 or one million
2. 672,348   672,821   673,187   673,897   673,901
3. a) <   b) >
Challenge 2
1. 1,491,226 circled
2. a) 295,843   b) 3,528,910   c) 7,990,190
3. 1,034,543   1,034,765   1,034,792   1,035,023   1,035,256
Challenge 3
1. 2,075,000
2. 6,705,890 (Accept any digits in place of the zeros.)
3. 357 hundreds ticked

Page 23
Challenge 1
1. 602,470 circled
2. a) 214,642   b) 915,632
3. a) 381,700   b) 380,000
4. 15,798   16,498   15,598 circled
Challenge 2
1. a) 1,205,915   b) 3,611,200
2. a) two million, eight hundred and nine thousand
   b) seven million, one hundred and five thousand, eight hundred and thirty
3. a) 7,692,000   b) 8,000,000
Challenge 3
1. a) >   b) >   c) <
2. a) Accept any number bigger than 7,099,997 but smaller than 7,100,002

b) Accept any number bigger than 5,450,000 but smaller than 5,460,000
3. a) 5,899,995   b) 5,850,000   c) 5,895,000

Page 25
Challenge 1
1. a) −3   b) −7   c) −3   d) 2   e) 5   f) 2
2. −2 °C   3. −2 °C
Challenge 2
1. a) −8   b) −18   c) −15   d) 14   e) 12   f) 7
2. −9 and −21 circled   3. −7 and 8 both circled
Challenge 3
1. −4   2. −16   3. 7 °C
4. a) −11   b) 33   c) 13   d) 8

Page 27
Challenge 1
1. 1,200 (leaflets)   2. 648 (adults)
Challenge 2
1. 150,394 (people)
2. a) 13,209 (cars)   b) 20,885 (cars)
Challenge 3
1. 61,646 (beads)
2. a) 968 (people)   b) 58,796,742 (people)

Page 29
Challenge 1
1. a) 4,000   b) 12,000   c) 3,000
2. a) 77,654 − 23,782 (= 53,872) or 77,654 − 53,872 (= 23,782)
   b) 23,878 + 37,058 (= 60,936)
3. 1,128 + 6,902 = 8,030 (Accept 7,826 − 1,128 = 6,698)
Challenge 2
1. a) 30,000   b) 110,000   c) 30,000
2. 628,147 − 369,065 (= 259,082) or 628,147 − 259,082 (= 369,065)
3. 524 (boxes)
Challenge 3
1. a) 1,200,000   b) 1,100,000   c) 1,600,000
2. 1,810,131
   1,810,131 − 1,219,362 (= 590,769) or 1,810,131 − 590,769 (= 1,219,362)
3. An explanation that shows Amol is incorrect because the smallest 5-digit number is 10,000 and 10,000 × 5 = 50,000 **and** 50,000 is greater than 49,999

Page 31
Challenge 1
1. a) 48, 72 and 84 circled   b) 72 and 108 circled
2. 15   3. 51 circled
Challenge 2
1. a) 160, 300 and 420 circled
   b) 275, 325 and 550 circled
2. a) 30   b) 12   c) 12
3. a) 12   b) 12   c) 5
4. 2, 5, 13 or 2, 7, 11
Challenge 3
1. 30   2. a) 6   b) 60   c) 100
3. 26   4. Tuesday
5. Possible answers are: 11, 13, 17, 31, 37, 71, 73, 79, 97

Page 33
Challenge 1
1. a) 1,541   b) 6,592
2. a) 119   b) 23
3. a) 24   b) 433
4. 56

Challenge 2
1. a) 6,604   b) 62,016
2. a) 16   b) 303
3. a) 191   b) 106
4. Explanation that shows multiples of 25 or numbers divisible by 25 will have 00, 25, 50 or 75 as the final two digits.

Challenge 3
1. a) 52,544   b) 166,110   c) 182,592
2. a) 203   b) 230   c) 205
3. a) 67   b) 278   c) 32
4. 7,052

Page 35
Challenge 1
1. 1,536 (cans)   2. 233,928 (passengers)
3. a) 30   b) 40   c) 180
Challenge 2
1. 373 (pencils)   2. 1,124
3. a) 1,500   b) 3   c) 165
Challenge 3
1. 8,016
2. a) 4,000   b) 50,100   c) 488
3. a) $(40 + 40) \times (20 + 20) = 3,200$
   b) $(120 - 60) \times 2 + (120 \div 10) = 132$

Pages 36–39
Progress test 2: maths
1. a) 57,200   b) 4,999   c) 15,000   d) 16
   e) 90,909   f) 9,999
2. 3,732,767   3,734,189   3,876,034   3,876,155
   3,876,210
3. 41; 56; 32
4. 22,186 (runners)
5.

4,930,000	5,000,000	4,925,200
2,180,000	2,000,000	2,184,750

6. 5,841,986 circled
7. 36
8. a) 9 °C   b) 0 °C
9. a) 56,000   b) 120
10. a) 2,306,051   b) 5,072,410
11. 115 (boxes)
12. 506,678
13. 72
14. 14,357 (tickets)
15. 9,802 (teddy bears)
16. −2
17. 1,500 (cabins)
18. 900,000 or nine hundred thousand
19. 99,900
20. 180 (seconds) or 3 (minutes)
21. 6 (teams) of 41 (children)
22. a) 3 + 37 or 11 + 29 or 17 + 23
    b) 2 + 7 + 31
23. a) $5,463 \times 36 = 32,778 + 163,890 = 196,668$
    b) $3,167 \times 27 = 22,169 + 63,340 = 85,509$
24. 45,450
25. five million, forty thousand and three hundred
26. a) $(80 - 60) \times 40 + 20 = 820$
    b) $300 \div (30 + 30 - 50) = 30$
    c) $(100 - 5^2) \times (100 - 90) = 750$
    d) $10^2 \div (40 + 10) \times (10^2 - 90) = 20$
27. 3 (trays)
28. a) 2,744   b) 4,770   c) 3,205

ENGLISH
Page 41
Challenge 1
1. a) tolerant   b) confident   c) expectant
   d) assistant   e) contestant   f) patient
Challenge 2
1. Each answer must use the correct spelling of the given word and demonstrate an understanding of the meaning of that word. Examples:
   a) There was no **urgency** to finish the work.
   b) There is a **vacancy** in the school office.
   c) She had a difficult **pregnancy**.
   d) His results showed **consistency**.
Challenge 3
1. Each answer must use the correct spelling of the given word and demonstrate an understanding of the meaning of that word. Examples:
   a) She speaks Spanish with wonderful **fluency**.
   b) The family took up **residency** in Spain.
   c) Her job was at risk of **redundancy**.
   d) Their life jackets gave them **buoyancy**.
2. a) innocence   b) ignorance   c) confidence
   d) contestant   e) consultant   f) triumphant

Page 43
Challenge 1
1. a) preferred   b) difference   c) transferring
   d) referring   e) referee   f) preferring
Challenge 2
1. Each answer must demonstrate an understanding of the meaning of the given word. Examples:
   a) I like coffee **though** I prefer tea.
   b) They walked **through** the forest.
   c) They gave the house a **thorough** clean.
   d) He **bought** some bread from the shop.
   e) He **brought** some bread to feed the ducks.
Challenge 3
1. a) unquestion**ably**   b) divis**ible**
   c) poss**ibly**   d) applic**able**
   e) terr**ibly**   f) uncontroll**able**

Page 45
Challenge 1
1. chief, ceiling, height, piece, vein, reindeer, beige, neighbour, deceive, thief, weight, mischief.
   chief, ceiling, piece, deceive, thief, mischief circled
Challenge 2
1. a) believe ✓ conceive ✓ perceive ✓ seize ✓
   b) receive, deceit, protein, ceiling
Challenge 3
1. a) Answer should acknowledge that i comes before e except after c if the vowels ie/ei make an ee sound (as in 'peep').
   b) Examples:
      We played in the field that was full of tall grass.
      I needed my receipt to get a refund.

Page 47
Challenge 1
1. a) whether   b) pouring   c) led   d) steel
Challenge 2
1. a) break   b) sum   c) passed   d) practised
Challenge 3
Each answer must demonstrate an understanding of the meaning of the given word.
1. Examples:
   a) The school principal led the assembly.
   b) He was a man of principle and would not change his mind.

2. Examples:
- **a)** I rode my horse.
- **b)** We rowed the boat down the river.

3. Examples:
- **a)** I accept that the accident was my fault.
- **b)** Everyone, except Tom, went to the party.

4. Examples:
- **a)** I decided to take her advice.
- **b)** He will advise them not to go.

Page 49
Challenge 1
1. **a)** adjective **b)** noun **c)** pronoun
2. **a)** verb and noun **b)** verb and noun

Challenge 2
1. Examples:
complement – something that goes well with something else
compliment – praise or congratulations
prophecy – a prediction of the future
prophesy – to say that something will happen
wary – feeling cautious about something
weary – feeling very tired

Challenge 3
1. Examples: deceive – cheat, trick, fool
receive – get, accept, obtain
seize – take, catch, grab
2. Examples: many – several
big – huge
buildings – constructions
grow – rise

Page 51
Challenge 1
1. *prim-* – first – primary; *ex-* – out – expel; *audi-* – hearing – auditory; *aqua-* – water – aquarium

Challenge 2
1. Each word to be used correctly in a sentence. Examples:
- **a)** There was a new machine in the factory.
- **b)** I bought a chandelier for the hallway.
- **c)** It was a unique picture.
- **d)** The instructions were a bit vague.

Challenge 3
1. Examples: **a)** photograph, graphics
b) microscope, microphone **c)** television, telephone
d) telescope, stethoscope **e)** photograph, photosynthesis
2. Each answer must use the correct spelling of the given word and demonstrate an understanding of the meaning of that word. Examples:
- **a)** I took a photograph.
- **b)** We looked at bugs under the microscope.
- **c)** She saw Saturn through the telescope.
- **d)** The doctor used a stethoscope.
- **e)** Plants use a process called photosynthesis.

Page 53
Challenge 1
1.
- Five European Championship gold medals
- Six World Championship gold medals
- Four Olympic gold medals

Challenge 2
1. **a)** Answer should acknowledge that the paragraph addresses the reader directly using 'you'. It also helps make them feel special and important.
b) Rhetorical questions. The answer should acknowledge that they are used to make the reader think about important points in the argument against the company and factory.

Challenge 3
1. **a)** Any three from:
dirty, noisy, smelly and polluting (one phrase)
irresponsible
no respect for the environment
even less for residents
The answer could also use the words 'promised' and 'financial reward' if they are mentioned as having the inverted commas around them to suggest that they are unlikely.
b) Answer should acknowledge that the introduction to the quote reminds the reader that this person is much respected (inferring that he can be trusted) and local (one of them). The quote itself is about how bad the company is and so supports the argument against them.

Page 55
Challenge 1
a) 3 **b)** 1 **c)** 2

Challenge 2
1. The cyclist has a coach. The coach is in a car.
2. Example: "I can't walk through this thick undergrowth," complained Joe. "And the thorns are scratching me."
"I know. It's almost impossible with these vines tangling around our feet. It's getting too dark to see," said Eve.

Challenge 3
1. The written text should give some information about the characters in the setting of a fairground ride, with descriptions about what is happening and how they are feeling. Example:
They stepped onto the ride and sat down. "I feel sick already," said Beth.
Clio stared ahead. "It's ok," she replied, nervously. Suddenly, they were off and spinning round at great speed before Beth let out her first of many screams of "Get me off here!"
"Yeeeessss!" squealed Clio, laughing as the ride shot up high into the air.

Page 57
Challenge 1
1. **a)** **B** ✓
b) Two from: <u>Racing along</u> – shows how fast the car was going; <u>before</u> – links two actions of the car; <u>Without warning</u> – shows that the following action was sudden; <u>then</u> – time connective linking the previous action to this action; <u>and</u> links the two actions

Challenge 2
1. The ellipsis could be placed after 'the ground gave way…' to add suspense, making the reader think AJ may have fallen.

Challenge 3
1. Example: All the way home from football, Noah cried. He was upset **because** he didn't score a goal today. His mum said it wasn't all about scoring goals **but** to Noah it was. **Once they arrived** at home, his mum gave him some chocolate to cheer him up. He loved chocolate **and**, feeling happier again, he went into the garden to practise scoring goals.

Page 59
Challenge 1
a) Wimbledon – a famous tennis tournament
b) All England Tennis Club, Wimbledon, London
c) End of June each year

Challenge 2
1. The précis should cover the points listed in the answer to Challenge 1 and the fact that the winners receive over £2 million. (1 mark for each point)

Example:
The famous Wimbledon tennis tournament is played every June at the All England Tennis Club, London. The male and female singles champions win over £2 million each as well as potential sponsor money.

Challenge 3

1. The précis should be a concise summary of the text, without superfluous information.

Pages 60–63 Progress Test 3: English

1. Examples:
   a) confident b) tired c) challenging
   d) rejected e) rewarded f) weak
2. a) transference b) deferral c) suffering
   d) conference e) preferring
3. a) aisle b) bridal c) bared
   d) stationary e) weather f) rode
4. List must be introduced with a colon (for 1 mark)
   Bullet point list following the colon (for 1 mark). Example:
   Janey's jobs:
   • Homework
   • Pack PE bag
   • Feed cat
   • Hang out the washing
   • Clean the kitchen
   • Tidy her bedroom
5. Examples:
   a) The bird tweeted.
   b) The fireworks fizzed and crackled.
   c) There was a bright flash of lightning.
6. Each word must be used appropriately in a grammatically correct sentence. Examples:
   a) The teacher said she was very observant.
   b) They were hesitant when they got to the edge of the water.
   c) The dog was very obedient.
   d) The monster was covered in a slimy substance.
7. Examples:
   a) thorough – careful, accurate, detailed
   b) thought – idea, reflection, contemplation
   c) rough – bumpy, coarse, rugged
8. Examples:
   a) led: past tense of the verb 'to lead'
   b) lead: verb 'to lead' – take the lead, lead people; or noun – a lead or the element lead
   c) desert: noun – a very dry area; or verb – to desert, which means abandon
   d) dessert: a sweet course at the end of a meal
   e) mourning: sorrow following a death
   f) morning: the part of the day before noon
9. The written text should give some information about the characters and the setting, with ideas about what they are doing and how they are feeling. It must include dialogue. (1 mark for description of the two characters; 1 mark for description of the house; 1 mark for dialogue).
   Example:
   "Let's get out of here," sobbed Sam gripping Amy's arm. Sam was only 6 and was nervous and scared. "We can't go that way past all the spiders," whispered his older sister, Amy, "Or through that door where the skeletons are." She tried to keep a straight face. It was fun teasing her brother. "Please get us out of here Amy!" he cried. Sam wished he'd never agreed to go to the fair, never mind go in the Haunted House.
10. a) Any three from: carefully, without a sound, before, only then
    b) stepped, slowly, softly
    c) she is scared/nervous and careful

11. a) … like a herd of huge elephants.
    b) … gentle waves licked the shore.
    c) birds crowed and cawed
12. a) Haiku b) stunning sky is still
13. a) employ b) faith c) caution d) cover

MATHS
Page 65
Challenge 1

1. $\frac{2}{3} = \frac{4}{6} = \frac{6}{9} = \frac{8}{12} = \frac{10}{15} = \frac{12}{18}$
2. a) $\frac{3}{4}$ b) $\frac{5}{8}$ c) $\frac{7}{10}$
3. $\frac{7}{12}$ $\frac{2}{3}$ $\frac{3}{4}$ $\frac{5}{6}$ (Accept $\frac{7}{12}$ $\frac{8}{12}$ $\frac{9}{12}$ $\frac{10}{12}$)

Challenge 2

1. a) $\frac{4}{5}$ b) $\frac{11}{15}$
2. a) $\frac{3}{5}$ b) $\frac{3}{7}$
3. $\frac{9}{15}$ $\frac{2}{3}$ $\frac{7}{10}$ $\frac{4}{5}$ (Accept $\frac{18}{30}$ $\frac{20}{30}$ $\frac{21}{30}$ $\frac{24}{30}$)

Challenge 3

1. a) $\frac{2}{9}$ b) $\frac{3}{4}$ c) $\frac{1}{3}$ d) $\frac{3}{16}$
2. a) $\frac{5}{9}$ $\frac{7}{12}$ $\frac{2}{3}$ $\frac{3}{4}$ (Accept $\frac{20}{36}$ $\frac{21}{36}$ $\frac{24}{36}$ $\frac{27}{36}$)
   b) $\frac{3}{5}$ $\frac{2}{3}$ $\frac{3}{4}$ $\frac{5}{6}$ (Accept $\frac{36}{60}$ $\frac{40}{60}$ $\frac{45}{60}$ $\frac{50}{60}$)
3. a) $\frac{17}{20}$ b) $\frac{29}{72}$ c) $\frac{13}{60}$

Page 67
Challenge 1

1. a) $\frac{7}{8}$ b) $\frac{7}{10}$ c) $\frac{11}{12}$
2. a) $\frac{4}{10}(=\frac{2}{5})$ b) $\frac{5}{12}$ c) $\frac{1}{12}$
3. $\frac{1}{2}$ (of the cakes)

Challenge 2

1. a) $\frac{9}{20}$ b) $5\frac{1}{40}$ c) 7
2. a) $\frac{13}{20}$ b) $\frac{4}{15}$ c) $\frac{5}{12}$
3. $1\frac{15}{24} = 1\frac{5}{8}$ (more of the mushroom pizza)

Challenge 3

1. a) $6\frac{7}{30}$ b) $9\frac{9}{20}$ c) $8\frac{3}{30}(=8\frac{1}{10})$
2. a) $1\frac{11}{20}$ b) $\frac{19}{24}$ c) $\frac{33}{40}$
3. $1\frac{1}{4}$ 4. $1\frac{4}{5}$ 5. $1\frac{9}{12}(=1\frac{3}{4})$

Page 69
Challenge 1

1. a) $\frac{1}{10}$ b) $\frac{1}{15}$ c) $\frac{1}{24}$
2. a) $\frac{1}{12}$ b) $\frac{1}{10}$ c) $\frac{1}{30}$
3. $\frac{3}{8}$ (of the pack)

Challenge 2

1. a) $\frac{2}{18}(=\frac{1}{9})$ b) $\frac{9}{20}$ c) $\frac{12}{50}(=\frac{6}{25})$
2. a) $\frac{3}{32}$ b) $\frac{5}{30}(=\frac{1}{6})$ c) $\frac{3}{24}(=\frac{1}{8})$
3. $\frac{7}{16}$ (of her homework)

Challenge 3

1. a) $\frac{1}{3}$ b) $\frac{1}{3}$ c) $\frac{2}{3}$
2. a) 5 b) 3 c) 4
3. $\frac{15}{8}(1\frac{7}{8})$ 4. $\frac{4}{15}$ (of the bag of flour)

Page 71

Challenge 1

1. a) 0.03 or $\frac{3}{100}$ or three hundredths

    b) 0.7 or $\frac{7}{10}$ or seven tenths

    c) 0.002 or $\frac{2}{1,000}$ or two thousandths

2. a) 0.51   b) 598   c) 2.619   d) 90.63

3. a) $\frac{90}{100}$ (= $\frac{9}{10}$) = 0.9   b) $\frac{35}{100}$ (= $\frac{7}{20}$) = 0.35

    c) $\frac{75}{100}$ (= $\frac{3}{4}$) = 0.75   d) $\frac{40}{100}$ (= $\frac{2}{5}$) = 0.4

Challenge 2

1. a) 0.207   b) 604   c) 0.431   d) 7.8

2. a) $\frac{15}{100}$ (= $\frac{3}{20}$) = 0.15   b) $\frac{12}{100}$ (= $\frac{3}{25}$) = 0.12

    c) $\frac{72}{100}$ (= $\frac{18}{25}$) = 0.72   d) $\frac{65}{100}$ (= $\frac{13}{20}$) = 0.65

3. 15%

Challenge 3

1. a) 10   b) 1,000

2. a) 0.4 = 40%   b) 0.96 = 96%

    c) 0.06 = 6%   d) 0.55 = 55%

3. 12.5% or $12\frac{1}{2}$%

Page 73

Challenge 1

1. a) 4.2   b) 3.6   c) 2.4   d) 0.28
2. a) 18.5   b) 8.2   c) 8.5   d) 15.75
3. 3.5 (kg)

Challenge 2

1. a) 0.72   b) 0.56   c) 4.5   d) 1.65
2. a) 173.5   b) 32.8   c) 55.75   d) 16.25
3. (£) 21.75

Challenge 3

1. a) 12   b) 9   c) 0.12   d) 0.02
    e) 15   f) 34
2. 4 (taxis)
3. a) $16.\overline{3}$ b) $14.\overline{16}$

Page 75

Challenge 1

1. a) (£) 1.25   b) (£) 5
2. a) 7 (cm)   b) 28 (cm)

Challenge 2

1. a) (£) 140   b) (£) 560   c) (£) 840
2. a) 12 (cm)   b) 24 (cm)

Challenge 3

1. a) 195 (cars)   b) 325 (cars)
2. 37.5 (cm)   3. 14 (cm)

Page 77

Challenge 1

1. a) 20   b) 20   c) 75
2. 40 (questions right)
3. a) 20 and 10   b) 40 and 10   4. 350 (ml)

Challenge 2

1. a) 18   b) 76   c) 168
2. (£) 16   3. a) 80 and 60   b) 140 and 210
4. (£) 67.50

Challenge 3

1. 225   2. 1 (mark)   3. butter: 300 (g);   sugar: 350 (g)
4. 720 (ml)

Page 79

Challenge 1

1. 5n = 45 circled
2. (£) 8
3. n = 3x + 1 circled

Challenge 2

1. a) $\frac{50}{n}$ = 25   b) 15n = 90
2. (£) 385
3. a) 28   b) 58

Challenge 3

1. n − 4 = 95   2. 73 (marks)
3. a) (n =) 8x − 1   b) (n =) 5x + 3

Page 81

Challenge 1

1. ⬜ = 29, ⬤ = 1

2. 1,200 (ml)

3. Possible answers could be: a = 7, b = 1; a = 8, b = 2; a = 9, b = 3; … Accept any three solutions with positive whole numbers, where a is 6 greater than b

4. (£) 10 + (£) 5 + (£) 5 + (£) 5 + (£) 5 and (£) 10 + (£) 10 + (£) 5 + (£) 5

Challenge 2

1. c = 12, d = 2 or c = 2, d = 12
2. 1 (m)
3. Possible answers are: e = 2, f = 21; e = 4, f = 18; e = 6, f = 15; e = 8, f = 12; e = 10, f = 9; e = 12, f = 6; e = 14, f = 3
4. Any two of these possible answers:
    pen costs 47 (p), pencil costs 11 (p)
    pen costs 44 (p), pencil costs 12 (p)
    pen costs 41 (p), pencil costs 13 (p)
    pen costs 38 (p), pencil costs 14 (p)
    pen costs 35 (p), pencil costs 15 (p)
    pen costs 32 (p), pencil costs 16 (p)

Challenge 3

1. g = 25, h = 5
2. (£) 5 × 3, (£) 10 × 1, (£) 20 × 2
3. Possible answers are: j = 2, k = 28; j = 4, k = 16; j = 5, k = 10; j = 6, k = 4
4. Each larger group has 7 children; each smaller group has 2.

Pages 82–85

Progress test 4: maths

1. a) 77   b) 315   c) 1,780   d) 13
2. 3,978 (people)
3. a) 890   b) 4,624   c) 205
4. $\frac{52}{65}$ circled
5. a) (£) 8.25   b) (£) 13.75
6. a) n − 12 = 34   b) $\frac{n}{8}$ = 64
    c) n + 56 = 78 (Accept 56 + n = 78)
    d) 16n = 896
7. a) 4,093,000   4,100,000   4,000,000
    b) 6,937,000   6,900,000   7,000,000
    c) 8,250,000   8,200,000   8,000,000
8. 450 (bulbs)
9. 2,605,070
10. 41 (°C)
11. 626,091   626,022   625,138   624,923   624,135
12. a) 36 and 108 circled   b) 16 and 32 circled
    c) 57, 77 and 87 circled
13. $\frac{3}{8}$ (of the whole pizza)
14. $\frac{2}{5}$ = 0.4 = **40%**

    $\frac{1}{20}$ = 0.05 = **5%**

    $\frac{1}{25}$ = **0.04** = 4%

    $\frac{23}{50}$ = **0.46** = 46%

15. (£) 6.40

16. a) 89   b) 35

17. a) 40,840   b) 2,506,780

18. a) $\frac{11}{12}$ b) $\frac{13}{24}$ c) $\frac{11}{12}$

19. a) 9,000   b) 42,000   c) 140

20. $\frac{3}{5}$ $\frac{5}{8}$ $\frac{13}{20}$ $\frac{27}{40}$ $\frac{7}{10}$ (Accept $\frac{24}{40}$ $\frac{25}{40}$ $\frac{26}{40}$ $\frac{27}{40}$ $\frac{28}{40}$)

21. 13.5 (m)

22. (£) 2,700

23. a) 12 (cm)   b) 42 (cm)

24. Kyle: (£) 60
    Javid: (£) 40
    Joe: (£) 20

25. a) £8.10   b) £8.60

26. Possible answers are:
    $a = 1, b = 17; a = 2, b = 13; a = 3, b = 9; a = 4, b = 5; a = 5, b = 1$

27. (£) 4.50

28. 30 (tables)

29. a) 8   b) 80   c) 0.05

30. $2\frac{1}{2}$ (litres)   (Accept $2\frac{4}{8}$ (litres) or 2.5 (litres))

31. a) $\frac{9}{10}$ b) $\frac{3}{5}$

ENGLISH
Page 87
Challenge 1
1. a) slight, tiny   b) trot, jog   c) furious, enraged
     d) toil, strive

Challenge 2
1. Reasonable antonyms should be given. Examples:
     a) light, bright   b) calm, relaxed
     c) dry, arid   d) cry, weep
     e) stand, rise   f) short, petite

Challenge 3
1. Reasonable synonyms should be given. Examples:
     a) peculiar   b) glared   c) strolled
     d) freezing   e) messy   f) intelligent
2. Each word must be matched with an antonym and both must be used in a grammatically correct sentence. Examples:
     a) hard – soft   The hard cricket ball hit the soft flesh of his arm.
     b) hot – cold   The hot drink was very welcome on such a cold day.

Page 89
Challenge 1
1. Examples:
     a) baked, was baked;   b) taught, was taught
     c) flew, was flown   d) drove, was driven

Challenge 2
1. a) active   b) passive   c) passive   d) active
     e) active   f) passive

Challenge 3
1. Examples:
    The dog was chasing the cat. (active)
      ⇧   ⇧
    Subject   Verb

    The dog was chased by the cat. (passive)
       ⇧   ⇧
    Subject   Verb

Page 91
Challenge 1
1. a) She **has** created a herb garden.
       She **had** created a herb garden before she went home.
     b) They **have** decorated the living room.

They **had** decorated the living room before they moved house.
     c) I **have** received a new bike.
       I **had** received a new bike when I last saw you.

Challenge 2
1. a) present perfect   b) past perfect
     c) present perfect   d) past perfect

Challenge 3
1. a) They have played football.
     b) I have showered.
     c) He has bought a new shirt.
     d) She has walked a long way.
2. a) They had danced to the music.
     b) We had swum in the sea.
     c) You had written a story.
     d) It had rained all day.

Page 93
Challenge 1
1. a) If I **were** you, I would try again.
     b) Dad asked that she **wash** the car.
     c) It was requested that he **finish** his homework.
     d) The officer instructed that the suspects **be** taken to the station.

Challenge 2
1. a) be   b) take   c) were   d) wear
2. a) put   b) hand   c) write   d) be

Challenge 3
1. I wish I <u>were</u> going on the trip with the others. Mr Jones requested that the pupils <u>be</u> at school by 8am and advised that they <u>be</u> picked up at 4pm. If I <u>were</u> going, I would make sure I <u>were</u> there very early.

Page 95
Challenge 1
1. proAmerican, exhusband, reevaluate, selfaware circled, and rewritten as: pro-American, ex-husband, re-evaluate, self-aware

Challenge 2
1. a) no   b) yes   c) no   d) yes
2. a) She had a little-used bike.
     b) We have two-year-old cousins.
     c) They saw the man-eating shark.
     d) We spotted the flower-destroying bugs.

Challenge 3
1. The response should acknowledge:
    Re-press means to press something again, e.g. 'Re-press the trousers because they are still creased.' Repress means to stop something, e.g. 'They had to repress the fear they felt inside.'
2. a) There are eight **ninety-year-old** trees in the **big forest**.
     b) His friend's **ex-wife** has just bought a beautiful **new home**.
     c) It wasn't possible **to re-enter** the museum once we had left.
     d) She loved going **water-skiing** when she went on her **summer holidays**.

Page 97
Challenge 1
1. a) no   b) yes   c) no   d) yes
2. a) The horse hurt its leg again; it was still weak from the last injury.
     b) Mum is getting a new car; her old car keeps breaking down.
     c) The two sisters are tall; in fact they are both taller than their big brother.

d) Billy likes dance classes at school; he has great balance and strength.

Challenge 2

1. **a)** They sat at a table overlooking the bay; ~~and~~ it was a fabulous view.
   b) The Queen waved from the carriage; ~~and~~ her loyal subjects cheered.
   c) We spent half the day in the library; ~~but~~ we could not find the book we wanted.
   d) There were lots of people singing; ~~although~~ I did not join in with my awful voice.
2. **a)** Maddie was hoping to visit a number of places on her trip: Barcelona, Spain; Lisbon, Portugal; Berlin, Germany; Paris, France and Venice, Italy.
   b) I had so much to do at the weekend including tidying my bedroom; doing all my homework; meeting my friends at the cinema; going to a football match with my dad; taking my sister to her dance class and helping with the gardening.

Challenge 3

1. The answer could acknowledge that the semi-colon allows both possibilities to exist at the same time. A full stop would show two separate 'times'.
2. The sentence should use semi-colons to separate long items in a list. Example: For Christmas, I would like some new white trainers; a pink biker jacket; a new game for my console and a selection of fruity bath bombs.

Page 99

Challenge 1

1. **b)** ✓   **d)** ✓

Challenge 2

1. **a)** ...from 1889–1895.
   b) ...that golden moment – silence.
   c) My mum's necklace – the one with the silver locket – is very precious.
   d) ...from 0800–1500...

Challenge 3

1. Examples:
   a) The explorers wanted just one thing – water.
   b) The Labrador – Marley's friend's dog – won the dog show.
   c) Harry went on holiday to Spain every year from 2005–2014.

Page 101

Challenge 1

1. **a)** ✓   **d)** ✓

Challenge 2

1. **a)** She did several events: throwing, jumping, running and cycling.
   b) His guitar was beautiful: the craftsmanship was of the highest quality.
   c) Every year we visit four places: the beach, the pier, the fairground and the beachside café.
   d) They reached the summit of the mountain: it was due to their excellent training plans.

Challenge 3

1. **a)** Their camping list included: a tent, sleeping bags, inflatable beds, a water carrier and a gas stove.
   b) The list must be introduced with a colon. Example: Camping list:
   - Tent
   - Sleeping bags
   - Inflatable beds
   - Water carrier
   - Gas stove

(Accept lower-case letters for each item too.) (1 mark for using the colon to introduce the list; 1 mark for using bullet points.)

2. Example: Kyle's racing bike has the following key features: a lightweight saddle, narrow tyres, an aerodynamic shape and special paint. (1 mark for using the colon to introduce the list; 1 mark for using commas.)

Pages 102–105
Progress test 5: English

1. Examples:
   a) lovely   **b)** icy   **c)** soar
   d) stiff   **e)** warmth
2. **a)** It was an incredible story – quite inspirational.
   b) The school library opens from 12:30–3 each day.
   c) Beside the tree – the one with the treehouse – we found a fossil.
   d) Queen Victoria lived from 1819–1901.
3. Examples:
   a) They made their descent of the mountain at first light.
   b) She showed her dissent to the plan.
4. **b)** ✓   **c)** ✓   **d)** ✓   **e)** ✓
   perceive, belief, seize, conceit
5. **a)** present perfect   **b)** past perfect
   c) present perfect   **d)** past perfect
6. **a)** hilarious, amusing   **b)** wealthy, affluent
   c) big, towering   **d)** unhappy, tragic
7. **a)** listen   **b)** attempt   **c)** were   **d)** be
8. **a)** It was an easy journey; the sea was calm.
   b) Their cake was judged to be the best; they were great bakers.
   c) Nobody could have guessed the ending; it was a total surprise.
   d) Eating in the restaurant was delightful; every dish was a masterpiece.
9. Example: Places to visit in London:
   - Trafalgar Square
   - Buckingham Palace
   - Big Ben
   - Tower of London
   - London Eye
   (1 mark for using the colon to introduce the list; 1 mark for using bullet points.)
10. Examples:
    a) The floorboards creaked and cracked.
    b) He crept along the path like a curious cat.
    c) His idea was a bright star of hope.
    d) The sun smiled down on us.
    e) The dew glistened on the green grass.
    f) This bag weighs a ton.
11. **a)** Example: Henry will meet his new pet. It might be a puppy.
    b) Any from: Finally, it was time to go home; grabbing his coat and bag; dashed outside; He sprinted out of the school grounds quickly; as he ran
    c) The afternoon had lasted forever.
    d) Any three from: Finally, forever, outside, quickly, already, excitedly
    e) Any three from: torrential, new, dirty, deep, little
12. They needed to sort out lots of things for the party including: booking a venue; finding a DJ; ordering the food; making a cake; buying the decorations and sending out invitations. (1 mark for using colon; 1 mark for using semi-colons correctly)
13. Example: Objects that could be found in a kitchen:
    - a fridge
    - an oven
    - a toaster
    - a kettle

- a microwave
- a sink

(I mark for using the colon to introduce the list; I mark for using bullet points.)

14. **a)** advice **b)** desert **c)** route **d)** quiet
15. **a)** Shivi created the book.
   b) The cake hadn't been eaten yet (by him).
   c) A phone call was made to my friend last night (by me).
   d) The window was broken yesterday (by the boys).
   e) My neighbour built the fence.

MATHS
Page 107
Challenge 1
1. **a)** 3,500 (m) **b)** 4,200 (g) **c)** 10,500 (ml)
2. **a)** 2.25 (m) **b)** 3.5 (litres) **c)** 0.125 (kg)
3. 40 (miles) (Accept answers +/− 1 mile)
4. 24 (kilometres) (Accept answers +/− 1 km)
Challenge 2
1. **a)** 10,750 (m) **b)** 4,020 (g) **c)** 1,005 (ml)
2. **a)** 0.25 (m) **b)** 0.305 (litres) **c)** 0.005 (kg)
3. 187.5 (miles) (Accept answers +/− 1 mile)
4. 1,403.2 (km) (Accept answers +/− 2 km)
Challenge 3
1. **a)** 25 (m) **b)** 10,025 (g) **c)** 12,150 (ml)
2. **a)** 0.125 (km) **b)** 0.005 (litres) **c)** 15.275 (kg)
3. 153 (km) (Accept answers +/− 1 km)
4. 2,868 (miles) (Accept answers +/− 5 miles)

Page 109
Challenge 1
1. 9 cm long, 1 cm wide; 7 cm long, 3 cm wide; 6 cm long, 4 cm wide; 5 cm long, 5 cm wide
2. 60 cm² **3.** 30 cm²
Challenge 2
1. Four answers to be given. Possible answers are:
   11 cm long, 1 cm wide; 10 cm long, 2 cm wide;
   9 cm long, 3 cm wide; 8 cm long, 4 cm wide;
   7 cm long, 5 cm wide; 6 cm long, 6 cm wide
2. Four answers to be given. Possible answers are:
   36 cm long, 1 cm wide; 18 cm long, 2 cm wide;
   12 cm long, 3 cm wide; 9 cm long, 4 cm wide;
   6 cm long, 6 cm wide
3. 300 cm² **4.** 500 cm²
Challenge 3
1. 4 (cm) **2.** 25.5 cm² **3.** 31.5 cm²
4. **a)** 98 cm (48 cm long, 1 cm wide)
   b) 23 cm² (23 cm long, 1 cm wide) **c)** 2 cm **d)** 30 cm

Page 111
Challenge 1
1. **a)** 1,920 cm³ **b)** 4,500 cm³
2. **a)** 256 cm³ **b)** 162 cm³ **c)** 350 cm³
   d) 240 cm³ **e)** 2,000 cm³ **f)** 729 cm³
Challenge 2
1. **a)** 216 cm³ **b)** 512 cm³
2. 58 **3.** 360 cm³
Challenge 3
1. Accept any three numbers that multiply to 240, e.g.
   240 cm long, 1 cm wide, 1 cm high
   120 cm long, 2 cm wide, 1 cm high
   60 cm long, 2 cm wide, 2 cm high
2. 1,250 cm³ **3.** 540 cm³

Page 113
Challenge 1
1. **a)** A, B and C **b)** B **c)** D
2. radius circled **3.** cube (Accept cuboid)

Challenge 2
1. Shape C and Shape D
2. **a)** 11.5 cm **b)** 8.25 cm
3. Net B circled
Challenge 3
1. trapezium circled **2.** length 20 cm, width 5 cm
3.

Page 115
Challenge 1
1. **a)** 109° **b)** 75° **c)** 134° **d)** 199° **e)** 156°
Challenge 2
1. **a)** 35° **b)** 55° **c)** 55° **d)** 158° **e)** 51° **f)** 46°
2. 120°
Challenge 3
1. **a)** 72° **b)** 210°
2. 57° and 48° **3.** 135°

Page 117
Challenge 1
1. (−1, 4), (2, 4), (−3, 0) and (4, 0) **2.** (0, 0)
3.

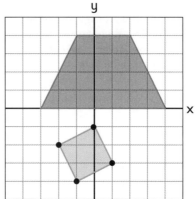

Challenge 2
1. **a)** (1, 1), (−3, 0) and (−2, −4) **b)** (2, −3)
2. **a)** and **b)**

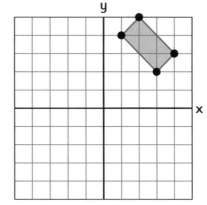

3. (4, 0) (Accept (−6, 5))
Challenge 3
1. (−1, −3)
   (5, −3)
   (−3, 1)
2. Accept any coordinates with 3 as the x-coordinate and the y-coordinate with any value of 2 or less. E.g. (3, 0) or (3, −1)
3. **a)** (−1, −1) **b)** (−1, 2)

Page 119
Challenge 1
1. **a)** Translated to A' (Coordinates (−2, 0), (0, 0), (−2, −1) and (0, −1)
   b) Translated to B' (Coordinates (2, 3), (2, 1) and (4, 1))

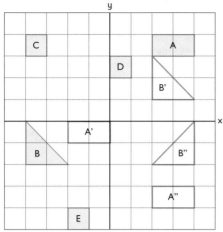

2. 4 squares right, 1 square down
3. a) Reflected to A" (Coordinates (2, −3), (4, −3), (2, −4) and (4, −4))
   b) Reflected to B" (Coordinates (4, 0), (2, −2) and (4, −2))

Challenge 2
1. a) 7 squares left, 1 square up
   b) 3 squares left, 3 squares up
2. a) Rectangle D to Rectangle C
   b) Rectangle D to Rectangle B
3. a) Translated to E' (Coordinates (−5, 3), (−3, 2), (−5, 0) and (−3, 1))
   b) Translated to F' (Coordinates (2, −1), (0, −2), (3, −2) and (2, −5))

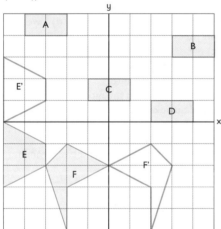

Challenge 3
1. a) 1 square right, 2 squares down
   b) 1 square right, 1 square up
2. Translated to D' (−2, −2), (−5, −3), (−3, −3) and −2, −5))
3. Reflected to E' (−3, −1), (1, −1), (−4, −2) and (0, −2)

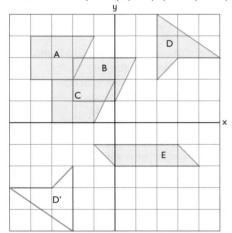

Challenge 1
1. a) 50 (guests)   b) 20 (guests)
   (Accept answers +/− 2 guests)
2. a) 152 (miles)   (Accept answers +/− 2 miles)
   b) 45 (minutes) (Accept answers +/− 2 minutes)

Challenge 2
1. 10 (guests)
2. a) 60 (miles) (Accept answers +/− 2 miles)
   b) A minimum of 30 (minutes)
      (Accept answers that state that it is only known that the car did not move between 2.00 p.m. and 2.30 p.m. The stopping time may have been earlier and the setting off time may have been later).

Challenge 3
1. 30 (guests)   2. 60°
3. An explanation that shows the only fixed points are 1:00 p.m. (0 miles) and 1:30 p.m. (20 miles). Points between these two times are unknown, so the actual starting point cannot be identified.

Page 123
Challenge 1
1. 122   2. 17   3. (£) 109 4. 13 and 14

Challenge 2
1. 37   2. 155 156 157   3. (£) 5.46 4. 1,080 (g)
   (Accept 1.08 kg)

Challenge 3
1. 43.5   2. 65   3. (£) 130   4. (£) 5.39

Pages 124–127
Progress test 6: maths
1.

 ✓

2. a) 6,500 (g)   b) 79 (mm)   c) 935 (cm)
   d) 3.975 (km)   e) 10.825 (litres) f) 8,025 (g)
3. a)

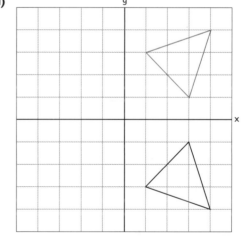

b)

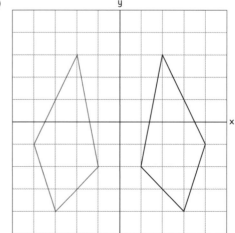

4. a) 118°   **b)** 146°   **c)** 307°   **d)** 45°
5. a) (£) 600   **b)** (£) 500
(Accept answers +/– (£) 25)
6. a) 24 (cm)
   b) Two answers to be given. Possible answers are:
   74 (cm)   (36 cm long, 1 cm wide)
   40 (cm)   (18 cm long, 2 cm wide)
   30 (cm)   (12 cm long, 3 cm wide)
   26 (cm)   (9 cm long, 4 cm wide)
7. a) 42 (cm²)   **b)** 75 (cm²)   **c)** 8 cm
8. 37.5 (miles)   (Accept answers +/– 2 (miles))
9. 25 (cm)
10. a) triangular prism and square-based pyramid
   b) triangular prism and cuboid
   c) NO circled. Explanation that states rectangular faces on a triangular prism and a cuboid can be square.
   d) NO circled. Explanation that states rectangular faces on a triangular prism and / or the square base on a square-based pyramid have right angles.
11. 17.5 (m)
12. 67.5 (%)
13. a) 70 (cm²)   **b)** 600 (cm²)
14. D circled
15. a)

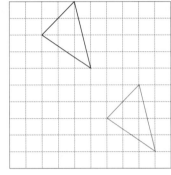

   b)

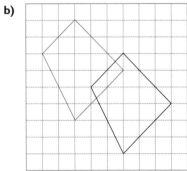

16. a) 48°   **b)** 34°
17. a) 120°   **b)** 144°
18. a) 140 (cm) (Accept answers +/– 5 (cm))
   b) 20 (cm)   (Accept answers +/– 5 (cm))

Pages 128–135 Mixed questions: English

1. a) not – when something is illegal it is against the law
   b) wrongly – misread means something read incorrectly
   c) opposite of / not – to disagree is to not agree
   d) not – to be not prepared
2. rattle, squeal, chatter
3. a) presidency   **b)** significance
   c) dominance   **d)** decency
4. a) steel   **b)** reins   **c)** bow
   d) male   **e)** cereal   **f)** insight
5. a) simile   **b)** personification   **c)** metaphor
   d) metaphor   **e)** personification   **f)** simile
6. a) School newsletter – B, Formal
   Diary entry – A, Informal
   b) Passage A: informal – e.g. models were dead boring
   Passage B: formal – e.g. … the pupils were fascinated…

c) Examples:
   'Lunch was taken' is more formal than 'we had lunch'.
   'the quality of the food was high' is more formal than 'the food was yummy'
   'Although not cheap' is more formal than 'it was a bit of a rip-off'
7. Examples:
   a) calm, tame   **b)** awful, dreadful   **c)** hate, dislike
   d) shout, yell
8. a) It represents the journey a stick takes as it floats along a stream and river and into the sea.
   b) drifting like a proud ship
   c) 'tossed' shows that the stream is rough, tossing the stick around, and 'drifting' shows that the river is more gentle.
   d) pollution
   e) Any two from: a stick, a stream; bigger sticks, branches and real boats; bags and bottles; the sea, surrounded by small fish.
   f) To make the reader wonder what happens next, and whether it is the start of a new adventure for the stick.
9. a) What? The River Amazon
   Where from? From its source in the Andes mountains.
   Where to? To the Brazilian coast and into the Atlantic Ocean.
   b) The précis should contain the main points but not superfluous information such as 'dense rainforests, teeming with life'.
10. a) We have cooked a lovely meal.
   b) She has found the hidden path.
11. a) paint   **b)** clean   **c)** be   **d)** were
12. ex-president, self-conscious, re-enter, pro-European
13. b) ✓   **c)** ✓   **d)** ✓
14. a) They needed the following ingredients: eggs, butter, flour, sugar and chocolate.
   b) It was a beautiful view: the mountains reflected in the surface of the lake.
   c) The team for the match is as follows: Devon, Jess, Molly, Khalid, Zac and Elsie.
   d) An incredible surprise awaited them: Grandma had come to visit from Australia.
15. Examples:
   a) manuscript, transcript
   b) chronological, synchronise
   c) aquatic, aquarium
   d) geography, geology
16. a) Example:
   48-mile long; joining the Atlantic Ocean with the Pacific Ocean; a journey which took up to 5 months longer.
   b) Answer should acknowledge that they are all important facts about the function of/reason for the Panama Canal.
   c) Example: A fact box giving the length of each of the top 5 longest canals.
17. a) The football match was won (by the best team).
   b) His games console was sold (by him).
   c) The police officer issued a speeding ticket.
   d) Mum's vase was smashed (by Emma).
   e) The suitcases were packed (by Syed).
18. Sentence A means that someone is asking whether they are going to visit Mike. In Sentence B, the comma means that Mike is being asked whether he is going to visit someone/somewhere.
19. I will go to visit my friend. ✓
20. a) my fingers, without gloves, felt like icicles; darting around like tiny fish in a tank
   b) Any two from: faster; bitterly; difficult; quickly
   c) Any two from: thin; heavy; aggressive; forceful; cold; unfamiliar; quiet; tired

d) a quiet, tired part of town that seemed to be clinging on to me, refusing to let me go.

e) looking and listening

21. a) heard **b)** advice **c)** lead **d)** allowed

22. Example: Billy rushed into the classroom **and** sat down at his desk. He took off his coat and took out his books **then** sat back relieved. **Just a moment later**, Mr Jewson strode into the room **with** a stern look on his face. The class went silent.

23. a) by

b) AABB ✓

c) the garden pales

d) blackbird

e) It means that there is another swallow and baby swallows that nest on the chimney of a cottage with the swallow.

Pages 136–143

Mixed questions: maths

1. a) 301 **b)** 180 **c)** 80 **d)** 877

2. C circled.

3. 4,405 (seats)

4. a) 4 °C **b)** Cardiff and Glasgow

5. a) $\frac{4}{5}$ **b)** $\frac{2}{3}$ **c)** $\frac{3}{5}$

6. 450,000

7. $\frac{1}{4}$ ✓

8. a) 340 **b)** 159,718

9. a)

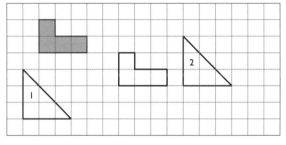

b) 10 squares right, 2 squares up

10. (£) 290,000

11. (£) 31

12. a) ▢ = 8 **b)** ◯ = 12

13. **2,439,157** circled

14. **C = 2r + 3** circled

15. 15,000   256,000   1,900,000   5,000,000

16. 12 (cm)

17. a) 8 and 20 **b)** 5 and 6

c) 5 and 11

18. a) 70

b) 40 + 50 ÷ (10 + 15) = 42

19. a) 60 (cm³) **b)** $\frac{1}{8}$ (of the planned cuboid)

20. a) 7.825 (kg) **b)** 42.5 (mm) **c)** 20,125 (m)

d) 12.575 (litres) **e)** 2.575 (km)

21. 46,080 (toy cars)

22. $\frac{7}{20}$

23. a) 40 (vans) **b)** 20 (buses)

c) 5 (buses) **d)** 35 (cars)

24. $\frac{1}{5}$ (of the bag)

25. $\frac{1}{5}$ = **0.2 = 20%**

$\frac{1}{4}$ = **0.25 = 25%**

$\frac{4}{5}$ = **0.8 = 80%**

$\frac{1}{20}$ = **0.05 = 5%**

26. a) 300 (cm²) **b)** 300 (cm²)

27. Accept any pentagon with three right angles, e.g.

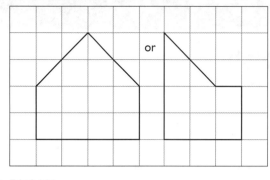

28. 7,063,406

29. 2 (kg)

30. a) 2 (°C) **b)** 10:00 **c)** 11 (hours) (Accept answers +/– 15 minutes) **d)** 2.5 (°C) (Accept answers +/– 0.2 °C) **e)** 4°C

31. NO circled. Explanation that shows an isosceles triangle can be right-angled if the angles are 90°, 45° and 45°. Accept a drawing to illustrate this.

32. a) (2, –1), (4, –1), (3,–2), (1, –4) and (4, –3)

b)

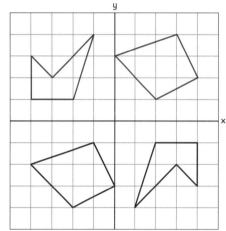

33. (regular) pentagonal-based pyramid

34. a) 90,000 **b)** 20,000

35. 187 (tins)

36. a) 8 **b)** 0.04 **c)** 0.4

37. $\frac{y}{5}$ – 15 circled

38. 5,787.5 (miles) (Accept answers +/- 50 miles)

39. a) Any three rows from:

Length	Width	Area
48 cm	1 cm	48 cm²
24 cm	2 cm	48 cm²
16 cm	3 cm	48 cm²
12 cm	4 cm	48 cm²

b) Any three rows from:

Length	Width	Perimeter
10 cm	1 cm	22 cm
9 cm	2 cm	22 cm
8 cm	3 cm	22 cm
7 cm	4 cm	22 cm
6 cm	5 cm	22 cm

40. 5 cm

41. x = 6, y = 2; x = 4, y = 5; x = 2, y = 8

Glossary

English

Active voice   In a sentence using the active voice, the subject of the sentence performs the action.

Adjective   A word used to modify nouns and proper nouns, e.g. colour, size or other features of an object or person.

Adverb   A word used to add more detail to a verb.

Adverbial phrase   A phrase used to add more detail to a verb.

Alliteration   The repetition of sounds in neighbouring or nearby words in a text. e.g. 'caught carelessly creating a commotion'.

Antonym   A word with an opposite meaning to another, e.g. happy and sad.

Bullet points   Used to break up information, usually making lists easier to read.

Cohesion   When sentences and paragraphs flow into each other, making writing more interesting and easier to read.

Colon   A punctuation mark used to introduce a list or speech in a playscript, or to separate two linked main clauses.

Comma   A punctuation mark used to separate items in a list, show different parts of a sentence, show parenthesis, and remove ambiguity.

Conjunction   A word used to join two sentences or parts of sentences, e.g. and, or, if, but, because, that, when.

Contraction   A word resulting from putting two words together and replacing the missing letter(s) with an apostrophe.

Dash   A punctuation mark used to highlight parenthesis or a pause in text, or to add extra related information.

Definition   The meaning of a word.

Dialogue   Speech.

Dictionary   A book containing an alphabetical list of words, with a definition of what each word means and what type of word/word class it is.

Ellipsis   A punctuation mark often used to imply suspense, made up of three dots.

Etymology   The origins and original meanings of words.

Fiction   Writing that is made up; not factual.

Figurative language   Words to suggest meaning by creating strong mental images for the reader.

Formal   Language that avoids slang words and is grammatically correct when spoken and written. It may include use of the subjunctive form of verbs.

Homophones   Different words with different spellings and meanings that sound exactly the same when spoken.

Hyperbole   Exaggerated statements used to emphasise a point and/or make the writing more interesting.

Hyphen   A punctuation mark sometimes used between a prefix and root word, or between words to avoid ambiguity.

Inference   Using ideas in a text to decide how or why something has happened, or how and why a character acts or feels in a certain way.

Infinitive form   The basic form of a verb, e.g. to be, to go, to walk.

Informal   A more casual way of sharing ideas and information. It uses contractions (e.g. can't) and may include slang words.

Main clause   A clause that can form a sentence on its own or with a subordinate clause.

Metaphor   Figurative language stating that something is something that it literally is not, e.g. 'a choir in the trees' to mean birds singing.

Morphology   How words are formed and relate to other words, e.g. through root words, prefixes and suffixes.

Near-homophones   Different words with different spellings and meanings that sound very similar when spoken.

Non-fiction   Writing using facts. Usually information texts such as a report, a recount or instructions.

Non-Standard English   Any form of English that is not Standard English.

Noun   The name of a person, place or thing.

Noun phrase   A word or group of words containing a noun and acting in a sentence as the subject or some type of object.

Object   Something that is acted upon by the subject in a sentence.

Onomatopoeia   A word that sounds like the sound associated with what the word is linked to, e.g. cuckoo, sizzle, whoosh.

Parenthesis   A word or phrase inserted into a text to give more information. Shown by brackets, commas or dashes.

Passive voice   In a sentence using the passive voice, the 'action' described by the verb is done to the subject.

Past participle   The form of a verb used to form the perfect tense, e.g. looked, walked.

Past perfect   Tense form that tells us that something had happened before something else.

Personification   Giving human characteristics to something non-human, e.g. the tree branches waved at us in the wind.

Poem   Writing that expresses ideas of feeling about someone or something, sometimes using rhyming words.

Précis   A summary of a text.

Prefix   Letter or letters added to the beginning of a root word that change the word's meaning.

Present perfect   Tense form that tells us that something has happened before the present (before now) but doesn't say exactly when it did happen.

Proper noun   A name given to a person, place or organisation; should always start with a capital letter, e.g. John, London.

Rhetorical question   A question often used in persuasive texts to make a point rather than to get an answer.

Rhyming pattern   The pattern with which words or lines rhyme in a poem.

Root word   A word before any further letters are added which alter the meaning, e.g. jump (which can become jumper, jumped or jumping).

Semi-colon   A punctuation mark used to separate two independent clauses without using a conjunction, or to separate longer items in a list.

Simile   Figurative language, when two objects are compared using similar characteristics. Usually contains the word 'as' or 'like'.

Glossary

Standard English   The form of English usually accepted as the correct form.

Subject   A person, place, thing or idea that is doing or being something.

Subject-specific vocabulary   Words used, particularly in non-fiction texts, which are specific to the topic or idea being discussed. Everyday use of these words is generally uncommon.

Subjunctive   Verbs have the final 's' removed in the subjunctive form, e.g. It is imperative that he **demonstrate** good behaviour. Used in formal speaking and writing.

Suffix   A letter or letters added to the end of a root word that change the word meaning.

Synonym   Words that have the same, or very similar, meanings to each other.

Thesaurus   A list of words and their synonyms, usually in alphabetical order.

Time connective   A word or phrase that refers to time and tells the reader when something happens.

Verb   Describes what the subject is 'doing', 'being' or 'having', e.g. She **reads** her book, I **am** tired, Zak **has** a new pen.

Word ending   Letter(s) at the end of a word.

Word family   A group of words that share similar spelling patterns or root words.

Maths

2-D   Describes shapes that have only two dimensions, usually described as length and width (or breadth). Sometimes 2-D shapes can have a height and a base.

3-D   Describes shapes that have three dimensions, usually described as length, width (or breadth) and height. These shapes exist in the real world and, if small enough, can be handled.

Acute angle   An angle that is smaller than a right angle, therefore less than 90°.

Angle   A turn around a point; measured in degrees.

Area   The amount of space inside a 2-D shape, measured using square units such as square centimetres (cm^2) or square metres (m^2).

Average   A middle value for a set of numerical data.

Base   The side a 2-D or 3-D shape 'stands' on.

BIDMAS   A reminder of the order of operations in a calculation involving two or more operations: **B** (Brackets) **I** (Indices) **D** (Division) **M** (Multiplication) **A** (Addition) **S** (Subtraction). BIDMAS is sometimes noted as **BODMAS**. The 'O' stands for 'of' – another term for multiplication – 4 (lots) of 2 = 8. It may also stand for 'order' or 'order of operations'.

Circumference   The outside edge or perimeter of a circle.

Common factor   4 is a factor of 20 and it is also a factor of 36, so 4 is a common factor of 20 and 36. Other common factors of 24 and 36 are 1, 2, 3, (4), 6, 12. (12 is the largest common factor and so is called the **highest common factor** or the **greatest common factor**.)

Common multiple   If a number is a multiple of two or more numbers then it is a common multiple of these numbers: 24 is a common multiple of 4 and 6. Other common multiples of 4 and 6 are: 12, (24), 36, 48 … . (12 is the lowest of these multiples and is called the **lowest common multiple**.)

Constant   In a formula, some numbers remain the same. These are constants, e.g. the formula for finding the perimeter of a rectangle is P = 2(l + w). The length (l) and the width (w) of a rectangle may vary, but once they have been added, the total is always multiplied by 2, so 2 is a constant.

Continuous data   Data or information that must be presented in order, often order of time. Temperature is continuous data as it varies. Continuous data is often represented as a line graph.

Coordinate grid   A square grid with vertical and horizontal lines. The lines are numbered and are used to find the coordinates of a point where the lines cross.

Cubic centimetres, cubic metres   Cubes that have a unit measure, so a cubic centimetre has sides of 1 centimetre, a cubic metre has sides of 1 metre.

Decimal   Our number system, based on groups of ten; decimal means counting in tens. Usually decimals or decimal numbers refer to numbers with a decimal point.

Decimal notation   A term used to describe our number system based on groups of ten, e.g. 10 tenths = 1 one, 10 ones = 1 ten.

Decimal place (dp)   The position of a digit used in a number to the right of the decimal point. The first digit after the decimal point has the 1st decimal place, the second number the 2nd decimal place and so on.

Decimal point A point, like a full stop, used in decimal numbers to separate whole numbers from parts of whole numbers.

Denominator The number below the dividing line in a fraction, showing the number of parts the whole is divided into.

Diameter A straight line from a point on the circumference of a circle, through the centre of the circle to a point on the opposite side of the circumference.

Division Sharing a number into equal groups; dividing by 4 shares the number into four equal groups, e.g. $16 \div 4 = 4$, there are four equal groups of 4. Also, a way of counting back in steps and knowing the number of backward steps, e.g. $8 \div 3 = 2$ r 2.

Equivalent fraction Equivalent fractions have the same value, e.g. $\frac{2}{5} = \frac{4}{10} = \frac{6}{15} = \frac{8}{20} \cdots$

Estimation A rough calculation of the value, number or extent of something, based on facts.

Factor A number that is multiplied to get another number. $4 \times 5 = 20$, so 4 and 5 are factors of 20.

Formula An abbreviated set of instructions to complete a calculation.

Fraction When a whole, whether it is an amount, a shape or a number, is divided into equal parts, each part is a fraction of the whole. A fraction is one number but is made up of two parts separated by a dividing line.

Height The height of a 2-D or a 3-D shape is the furthest perpendicular point from the base of the shape.

Imperial measures An older system of measures used before **metric measures** were adopted. Some are in length (inches, feet, yards, miles), in mass (ounces, pounds, stones) and in capacity (pints, gallons).

Improper fraction A fraction that represents a number that is a whole or is greater than a whole, e.g. $\frac{6}{5}$ is greater than one whole.

Interior angle An angle inside a 2-D shape.

Intersecting Describes lines that cross each other.

Inverse operation An operation that reverses another operation, e.g. subtraction is the inverse of addition; division is the inverse of multiplication.

Linear sequence A sequence of numbers. The numbers in a sequence are called 'terms' and any number in the sequence would be the 'nth term'.

Line graph A graph that shows a line or lines that display continuous information, often over a period.

Line of reflection The line over which a shape is flipped so it can be reflected. Also known as the **mirror line**.

Line of symmetry An imaginary or physical line that divides a shape into two equal parts that are a reflection of each other. Shapes can have more than one line of symmetry.

Long division A written method of recording a division. It records each step of the calculation in full, including calculation of remainders needed within the calculation.

Long multiplication A way of completing multiplication in written form, often with larger numbers set out in columns. It is described as a formal method. It records each individual multiplication of each pair of digits.

Mean 'Sharing out' of the numbers. The numbers in a set of data are added and the total divided by the number of numbers added. A type of average.

Median The middle number in a set of data that is ordered by size. A type of average.

Metric measures A system of measures based on groups of 10 units. The basic units are metre (length), kilogram (mass) and litre (capacity).

Mirror line See **line of reflection**.

Mixed number A whole number written with a fraction, e.g. $\frac{6}{5} = 1\frac{1}{5}$ This is a mixed number.

Mode The most commonly occurring number in a set of data. A type of average.

Multiple The answer when two whole numbers are multiplied, e.g. $4 \times 6 = 24$, so 24 is a multiple of 4 and 6

Multiplication An operation; a way of making repeated additions, e.g. $4 \times 3 = 4 + 4 + 4 = 12$

Negative number A number less than zero, e.g. -7.

Net A 2-D representation of the faces of a 3-D shape laid out as though the shape has been 'opened up' and laid flat. The edges of the 3-D shape remain connected.

nth term Used to describe any number in a sequence.

Numerator The number above the dividing line in a fraction and shows the number of parts being dealt with.

Numerical data Data using numbers.

Obtuse angle An angle larger than a right angle, therefore more than 90°, but smaller than a straight angle, therefore less than 180°.

Operation A mathematical process; the most common are addition, subtraction, multiplication and division.

Parallel Lines of 2-D shapes that are always the same distance apart, or faces of 3-D shapes that also remain the same distance apart.

Partition To break a number up into smaller parts so it is easier to work with. It can be done using place value, or by breaking a number up in other ways, e.g. $846 = 700 + 146$ or $846 = 500 + 300 + 46$.

Per cent Literally means 'out of 100'. A percentage is a special type of fraction that shows the number of parts per hundred or as hundredths. The symbol is %.

Perimeter The length of the outside edge of a shape, usually measured in centimetres (cm) or metres (m).

Pie chart A chart in the form of a circle where the 'pieces of pie' (sectors) show the relative sizes of data.

Place holder A digit used to make sure another digit appears in the correct column.

Place value The value of a digit according to its position in a number, e.g. in the number 285, the digit 8 has a place value of eight tens or 80 because it is in the tens column.

Power of 10 Powers of 10 are numbers achieved by multiplying 10 by itself twice or more, for example, $10 \times 10 = 100$ and $10 \times 10 \times 10 = 1{,}000$. 100 and 1,000 are powers of 10.

Prime number A number that is greater than 1 that cannot be made by multiplying two whole numbers together apart from multiplying by 1 and the number itself.

Proper fraction   A fraction with a numerator that is less than the denominator, e.g. $\frac{3}{8}$ or $\frac{9}{10}$.

Proportion   Proportion keeps ratios the same, so the ratio 1 : 3 is the same as 2 : 6, 3 : 9 and 4 : 12 and so on.

Quadrant   A coordinate grid that shows positive and negative numbers; is divided by the x-axis and the y-axis into four sections or quadrants.

Radius   A straight line from the centre of a circle to the circumference.

Ratio   The relative sizes of two or more amounts. A ratio is written with numbers separated by a colon, e.g. 3 : 1 means for every three there is one.

Recurring   A recurring decimal has a number or numbers that repeat indefinitely. To show the number is repeating, a bar or a dot is drawn above the repeating number, e.g. 6.333333... is shown as $6.\underline{3}$ or $6.\dot{3}$; 6.121212... is shown as $6.\overline{12}$ or $6.\dot{1}\dot{2}$

Reflection   A shape viewed as if in a mirror or as if it has been flipped over.

Regular polygon   Any 2-D shape with straight sides, where the sides and angles are all equal.

Right angle   An angle of 90°. It is a quarter turn.

Scale factor   A number that can be used to multiply or divide two or more numbers to keep them in the same proportion, e.g. a rectangle that measures 10 cm by 6 cm can be enlarged by a scale factor of 2, so that the measurements become 20 cm (10 × 2) by 12 cm (6 × 2).

Short division   A written method of division that allows for mental calculation of remainders.

Similar   Two shapes are similar following a transformation, that is after a reflection or translation, or if they have been re-sized by making them larger or smaller. The angles of these shapes remain the same although the length of sides and orientation can alter.

Simplest terms   When a fraction is reduced to its lowest or simplest terms, it means that the digits used are as small as possible. (Also known as lowest terms.)

Simplify   To reduce a number to its **simplest terms**.

Square centimetre, square metre   Squares that have a unit measure; a square centimetre has sides of 1 centimetre and a square metre has sides of 1 metre.

Substitution   In a formula, some numbers are variable and could be any number, but once they become known then they can be substituted into the formula, e.g. the formula to find the area of a rectangle is A = l × w (Area = length × width). If the length is 10 cm and the width is 6 cm, then the calculation to find the area becomes 10 cm × 6 cm (= 60 cm²).

Translation   The movement of a shape horizontally or vertically; it can be called a 'slide'. As the shape moves, it remains the same size and stays in the same orientation.

Trend   Data is plotted on a graph and can be joined by a line. The line that joins these points shows the trend. Points along the line may not be accurate.

Unknown   In an equation, a number is unknown if it is not actually shown, e.g. in the equation 6 + n = 10, n is the unknown, but it cannot be any number. Here, n must be 4.

Variable   In a formula, a variable stands for any number and it may vary, e.g. the formula to find the area of a rectangle is A = l × w (Area = length × width). The length and the width could be any measurement and so are variable. When these become known, they are substituted into the formula.

Vertex (pl. vertices)   The corner of a shape. In 2-D shapes, it is where two sides meet, and in 3-D shapes, it is where three or more edges meet.

Volume   The amount of space inside a 3-D shape. Volume of shape is measured in cm³.

x-axis   The line on a coordinate grid that runs horizontally.

y-axis   The line on a coordinate grid that runs vertically,.

Acknowledgements

The authors and publisher are grateful to the copyright holders for permission to use quoted materials and images.
All images are ©Shutterstock.com and ©HarperCollins*Publishers*
Every effort has been made to trace copyright holders and obtain their permission for the use of copyright material. The authors and publisher will gladly receive information enabling them to rectify any error or omission in subsequent editions. All facts are correct at time of going to press.
Published by Collins
An imprint of HarperCollins*Publishers*
1 London Bridge Street
London SE1 9GF
HarperCollins*Publishers*
Macken House, 39/40 Mayor Street Upper,
Dublin 1, D01 C9W8, Ireland
ISBN: 978-0-00-839882-8
First published 2020
10 9 8 7 6 5 4
©HarperCollins*Publishers* Ltd. 2020

All rights reserved. No part of this publication may be reproduced, stored in a retrieval system, or transmitted, in any form or by any means, electronic, mechanical, photocopying, recording or otherwise, without the prior permission of Collins.
British Library Cataloguing in Publication Data.
A CIP record of this book is available from the British Library.
Authors: Jon Goulding and Tom Hall
Publisher: Fiona McGlade
Project Development: Katie Galloway
Cover Design: Kevin Robbins and Sarah Duxbury
Inside Concept Design: Ian Wrigley
Page Layout: Q2A Media
Production: Karen Nulty
Printed in the United Kingdom by Martins the Printers

MIX
Paper | Supporting
responsible forestry
FSC™ C007454

Progress charts

Use these charts to record your results in the six Progress Tests. Colour in the questions that you got right to help you identify any areas that you might need to study and practise again. (These areas are indicated in the 'See page…' row in the charts.)

Progress test 1: English

	Q1	Q2	Q3	Q4	Q5	Q6	Q7	Q8	Q9	Q10	TOTAL /50
See page...	4	10, 8	4	4	6	14	4	8	8	12	

Progress test 2: Maths

	Q1	Q2	Q3	Q4	Q5	Q6	Q7	Q8	Q9	Q10	Q11	Q12	Q13	Q14	TOTAL /51
See page...	30, 28	20	30	26, 34	22	20	34	24	22	22	34	32	32	26, 34	
	Q15	Q16	Q17	Q18	Q19	Q20	Q21	Q22	Q23	Q24	Q25	Q26	Q27	Q28	
See page...	26, 34	34	26, 34	20	22	26, 34	26, 34	30	32	22	22	34	26, 34	32	

Progress test 3: English

	Q1	Q2	Q3	Q4	Q5	Q6	Q7	Q8	Q9	Q10	Q11	Q12	Q13	TOTAL /58
See page...	48	40	46	52	8	40	48	48	54	56, 8	8	12, 8	4	

Progress test 4: Maths

	Q1	Q2	Q3	Q4	Q5	Q6	Q7	Q8	Q9	Q10	Q11	Q12	Q13	Q14	Q15	Q16	TOTAL /71
See page...	30	26, 34	30, 32	64	74	80	22	26, 34	22	24	20	30	68	70	34	34	
	Q17	Q18	Q19	Q20	Q21	Q22	Q23	Q24	Q25	Q26	Q27	Q28	Q29	Q30	Q31		
See page...	20	66	22	64	74	76	74	74	78	80	78, 80	26, 34	30	26, 34, 70	66		

Progress test 5: English

	Q1	Q2	Q3	Q4	Q5	Q6	Q7	Q8	Q9	Q10	Q11	Q12	Q13	Q14	Q15	TOTAL /65
See page...	86	98	46, 48	44	90	86	92	96	52, 100	8	10, 8	96, 100	100	46	88	

Progress test 6: Maths

	Q1	Q2	Q3	Q4	Q5	Q6	Q7	Q8	Q9	Q10	Q11	Q12	Q13	Q14	Q15	Q16	Q17	Q18	TOTAL /40
See page...	112	106	118	114	120	108	108	106	108	112	112	76, 122	108	112	118	114	114	120	

Use this table to record your results for the Mixed questions sections on pages 128–143.

English mixed questions	Total score:	/ 109 marks
Maths mixed questions	Total score:	/ 89 marks